PRAISE FOR CURIOUS

"*Curious* is the most thoughtful, humane, deeply Christian perspective on drug use one could possibly imagine. It will now be a permanent part of my thinking. No Christian who cares about the drug crisis can ignore Christina Dent's remarkable testimony."

CORNELIUS PLANTINGA, PhD, Author
of *Under the Wings of God*

"If you've ever loved anyone with an addiction, stop what you are doing now, and read this beautiful and life-changing book. It's the most important thing you will do this year."

JOHANN HARI, Bestselling Author of
Chasing the Scream and *Stolen Focus*

"*Curious* is the perfect title for this book. As the statistics prove, whatever we have been doing in the last few decades is not working. This out-of-the-box work of Christina's heart and soul will engage your own heart and soul from the first page."

MARILYN TINNIN, Founder, Mississippi
Christian Living Magazine

"If we want better outcomes, we have to think outside the box. This book takes us there."

RYAN HAMPTON, Addiction Recovery Advocate and Bestselling Author of *American Fix* and *Unsettled*

"So good it could start a national movement."

REV. ALEXANDER SHARP, Founder, Clergy For a New Drug Policy

"Christina's story of her journey in *Curious* is compelling and gratifying. This is a must-read for everyone."

JEFFREY A. SINGER, MD, Senior Fellow, Cato Institute

"I met Christina while researching legislation to combat the drug epidemic in Mississippi. While you may or may not agree with all of the conclusions in this book, it certainly challenges us to explore creative approaches to curb illegal drug use and addiction. A beautifully written book."

SAM J. CREEKMORE IV, Mississippi House of Representatives

"Christina is an authentic and transformational leader who may change the way we confront the opioid epidemic."

ALAIN LITWIN, MD, MPH, Executive Director, Prisma Health Addiction Medicine Center

"I have been in law enforcement for over 42 years and was trained to know that drugs were illegal to sell, barter, manufacture, transfer, distribute or possess. This is all I have known and I've come to realize that it is a never ending fight with no winners. This book offers an opportunity to think about this issue from a different perspective and may be a catalyst for new ideas and strategies that produce positive results."

SHERIFF CHARLIE SIMS, Forrest County, Mississippi

"I encourage everyone to have an open mind and take this journey with Christina. Whatever your conclusions, you will learn. And learn. And learn."

BARRY FRIEDMAN, Director, Policing Project at New York University School of Law

"*Curious* stimulates out-of-the-box thinking beyond traditional approaches to addressing drug use."

GERARD GIBERT, Mississippi Entrepreneur

"Christina's approach to this nation's drug problem will challenge your assumptions and make you reconsider your preconceptions. Whether or not you agree with her conclusions, she will influence you to start forming your own."

HONORABLE LAWRENCE PRIMEAUX (RET.)

"*Curious* is a groundbreaking book for anyone willing to put aside old ideologies and focus on what will truly heal our broken world."

TIMOTHY MCMAHAN KING, Author of *Addiction Nation: What the Opioid Crisis Reveals About Us*

"A must-read for folks across the political spectrum because the extraordinary stories she tells will lead everyone to reflect on our values with open minds and hearts, considering how our society can best make progress on the challenges created by drugs and addiction."

PROFESSOR DOUGLAS A. BERMAN, Director, Drug Enforcement and Policy Center at The Ohio State University Moritz College of Law

"Books like *Curious* give me hope. At a time of heightened political tribalism, Christina reminds us that, with an open mind and a big heart, we can revisit contentious topics like how to handle drugs and we can find ways to better serve our communities."

BRAD LIPS, CEO, Atlas Network

"Christina takes us on a tour of the most sensitive and profound questions with love, mercy, and grace."

JIM HORTON, President, The Zachary Horton Foundation

"After a career in law enforcement, I'm convinced this book offers an important view of how we could treat drug use and addiction more effectively."

POLICE CHIEF BRENDAN COX (RET.), Director of Policing Strategies, LEAD Support Bureau

"Christina has captured and put words to the internal conflict many of us feel between anger and compassion on these issues. She takes us to possible solutions but honors each reader along the way and doesn't force us to accept them. *Curious* is a must-read for anyone wanting to understand the pros and cons of changing how we handle drugs and addiction, as well as anyone who worries about the future of our country and world."

JEFF GOOD, President, Mangia Bene Restaurant Management Group

"Christina's heart for others is contagious. I'm thrilled to see solutions being discussed that value the voices of people struggling with addiction. There may be no better investment in our country than to solve these issues."

JOSH BARTON, Executive Director, Home of Grace Addiction Recovery

"Drawing from major events in her personal life, Christina shares in a bold and vulnerable way. This is a book of great hope."

REV. DR. EDWARD TREAT, Founder & CEO, Center of Addiction & Faith

"Chock full of heart and hope, these pages help us see the dignity and humanity of every image bearer of God, and invite us to rethink our own orthodoxy when an approach fails to deliver on its promise. I hope you'll read this book."

GRANT CALLEN, Founder & CEO, Empower Mississippi

"Being a 34-year law enforcement professional, along with working as a college professor for 14 years, I fully understand and support the practical and theoretical perspectives outlined in Curious."

LIEUTENANT KEVIN D. LAVINE, Instructor of Criminal Justice, Jackson State University

"Christina nails it! We must stomp out the underground drug market, and this book shows us how to do it."

JOHN SHINHOLSER, President, The McShin Foundation

"Christina's curiosity manifests itself in a profound journey on a critical issue. After a career in policing and my own brother's overdose death, I took this journey myself and came to similar conclusions. This book shines a light on solutions grounded in compassion, empathy, and the sanctity of life."

LT. DIANE GOLDSTEIN (RET), Executive Director, Law Enforcement Action Partnership

CURIOUS

CURIOUS

A FOSTER MOM'S DISCOVERY OF AN
UNEXPECTED SOLUTION TO DRUGS AND ADDICTION

CHRISTINA DENT

Copyright © 2023 by End It For Good, Inc.

All rights reserved. No part of this book may be reproduced or transmitted in any form or by any means, electronic or mechanical, including photocopying, recording or by any information storage and retrieval system, without permission in writing from the copyright owner. For information on distribution rights, royalties, derivative works or licensing opportunities on behalf of this content or work, please contact the author.

Scriptures are taken from The ESV® Bible (The Holy Bible, English Standard Version®). ESV® Text Edition: 2016. Copyright © 2001 by Crossway, a publishing ministry of Good News Publishers. The ESV® text has been reproduced in cooperation with and by permission of Good News Publishers. Unauthorized reproduction of this publication is prohibited. All rights reserved.

Scripture quotations are taken from THE MESSAGE, copyright © 1993, 2002, 2018 by Eugene H. Peterson. Used by permission of NavPress. All rights reserved. Represented by Tyndale House Publishers, Inc.

Printed in the United States of America.

Although the author and publisher have made every effort to ensure that the information and advice in this book were correct and accurate at press time, the author and publisher do not assume and hereby disclaim any liability to any party for any loss, damage, or disruption caused from acting upon the information in this book or by errors or omissions, whether such errors or omissions result from negligence, accident, or any other cause.

To Joanne, You are the embodiment of courage.

To Thomas, We made it up the mountain because you cleared a path when I couldn't see the next step.

To Cole, Tyson, and Brandon, I delight in you. Always be open to learning something new.

TABLE OF CONTENTS

Introduction . . . . *xv*
Notes and Terminology . . . . *xix*

PART I: LIFE INTERRUPTED 1

Chapter 1: Loden Place .3
Chapter 2: Call The Police 11
Chapter 3: Mrs. Horton 15
Chapter 4: Invisible Wounds 19
Chapter 5: Until We Meet Again 27
Chapter 6: The Call 35
Chapter 7: Face to Face 41
Chapter 8: Going Home 47

PART II: LEARNING JOURNEY 53

Chapter 9: Rat Park 55
Chapter 10: Behind the Scenes 65
Chapter 11: A Fork in the Road 73
Chapter 12: We've Been Here Before 83
Chapter 13: The Wrong Winners 91
Chapter 14: The Flipside of Fentanyl 99
Chapter 15: Panorama 111

PART III: LASTING SOLUTIONS 119

   Chapter 16: Changing Course. 121

   Chapter 17: The Other War 129

   Chapter 18: Nuts and Bolts 137

   Chapter 19: Faith and Values 147

   Chapter 20: Our Kids 155

   Chapter 21: Stair Steps to Recovery. 161

   Chapter 22: Ingredients for Transformation. 175

   Chapter 23: Sober Another Way. 183

   Chapter 24: Two Thriving Lives 191

   Chapter 25: End It For Good 199

   Chapter 26: More Than You Might Think. 209

   Chapter 27: Small Big Things 219

Afterword *229*

Acknowledgments *235*

Notes *239*

About the Author. *241*

About End It For Good *242*

Spark Curiosity *243*

INTRODUCTION

I'm running on pure adrenaline at this point. Earlier today I led the largest event I've ever hosted, at the convention center in Hattiesburg, Mississippi. One hundred and twenty community leaders including the mayor, district attorney, sheriff, and several judges were in attendance. Now I just finished giving the same presentation to criminal justice students at the University of Southern Mississippi. As the students gather up their backpacks and head out into the cool November evening, the professor's wife walks up to me. She attended because she's an attorney, and sometimes drugs and addiction are part of the cases she works on related to children and families. She shakes my hand, gives a thoughtful smile and says, "You know, this is really a pro-life issue." I want to throw my arms around her neck and squeeze her tight. She understands the reason I'm here, the reason I'm starting a nonprofit and traveling around the state sharing this presentation. It isn't about drugs and addiction, it's about life. Lives. I'm here because of the *people* impacted by drugs, addiction, and how we approach those things.

Born, raised, and homeschooled in a Christian home in Jackson, Mississippi, my parents taught me to stay away from drugs, which was fine with me because I had no interest. The proverbial good girl, I never even smoked a cigarette growing up, much less used an illegal drug.

Continuing the same trajectory into college, I earned a degree in Bible from a Christian university, got married, and had kids. By the age of 30, I was a politically conservative, evangelical Christian mother who had checked all the expected boxes. I'm the last person you might think would be inviting people to consider seismic shifts to the way we've approached drugs and addiction for my entire lifetime.

But I became a foster mom, and through that experience, some pillars of my carefully ordered life were shaken. Joanne, the mother of one of our foster sons, was so different from me, and yet so much more alike than I wanted to admit. The more I got to know her, the more I began to question everything I thought I knew about drugs and addiction. I was left with a choice. Shut out what I could see with my own eyes, or start learning. Asking big questions and pursuing the answers with tenacity were ways of life that were deeply embedded in my home growing up, so I tried to swallow my pride, push pause on my fear, and get curious.

This book is the story of my life and paradigm shift as I rebuilt my knowledge and perspective on drugs and addiction from the ground up, learning from research and then seeing it lived out in the lives of people God brought into my path. You'll hear their stories too. What started as a desire to understand the birth mother of our precious foster son became a journey to discover which approach to drugs and addiction is most consistent with a comprehensively pro-life ethic. I'm not a doctor or policy expert, but laws and culture aren't just created by trained professionals. They're heavily influenced by regular people like you and me - people who can learn from professionals as well as our own experiences, and then take action in every community across the country. If there's a better path forward with drugs and addiction, and I believe there is, we'll be the ones to generate momentum towards it.

My unexpected journey led me to the TEDx stage and to founding a thriving nonprofit, but it started in an 800-square-foot house on a dead-end street in the heart of the Deep South.

NOTES AND TERMINOLOGY

All of the stories in this book are true according to journals, interviews, and my own memory and interpretation of events.

In this book I most often refer to Substance Use Disorder (SUD) as addiction. I realize that many people who work in the SUD and recovery fields have stopped using the term addiction, but I kept it here to avoid confusion for readers.

Names have been changed only when I was unable to reach someone for permission to include their story.

PART I:
LIFE INTERRUPTED

CHAPTER 1

LODEN PLACE

The screened door slams behind me as I bolt out the back of our house, past the huge ash tree with swings and rope ladders dangling from its branches, and through the backyard. The sound of kids' voices fills the mild Mississippi evening. Half are yelling in excitement and half are out for blood. The Little Kids just pulled one of our best pranks on the Big Kids, cutting electricity to their clubhouse. It has to be punished, of course, so the Little Kids are running for our lives as the Big Kids chase us. At 9 years old I'm the youngest of the Little Kids, but tall for my age and finally fast enough not to be the first person caught. Micah and Joel, my oldest brothers, are part of the Big Kids while my third brother, Daniel, and I are Little Kids. Of course, the Big Kids decide who belongs in which group. We have a close-knit community of friends who are homeschooled like we are, and even though none of them live in our neighborhood, their parents regularly drop them off for an evening of fun at our house. Like tonight.

My heart pounds with a mixture of fear and excitement as I cut through the neighbor's yard and sneak through the woods, briars snagging on my clothes. Ten yards ahead of me is The Barn, a real abandoned barn that our landlord allowed Dad and my brothers to turn into a clubhouse. Five minutes before, light was pouring through the cracks in the weathered siding of the loft, and the Christian music of Michael W. Smith and Amy Grant was floating out the open loft door. Now it's as dark as the night around me. I love a good game of chase, but some of the rough-housing when you get caught is a little more than I can handle. I'll hide here until the other Little Kids get caught and the adrenaline calms down.

Our house is the middle of three rental houses on a dead-end street. After the third house, the street turns into a gravel road passing through the woods where I'm hiding and in front of the old barn. When our family moved to this house, I was one year old. Dad had just graduated from Reformed Theological Seminary in Jackson, Mississippi, with two master's degrees - one in Old Testament and one in Christian Education. We moved 2 blocks down the road to 125 Loden Place so Dad could work at Mt. Salus Christian School in the neighboring town of Clinton. Loden Place wasn't the kind of house you'd think someone with two master's degrees would live in, though. Mom calls it "The Shoebox" because it's under 800 square feet. There's a kitchen and living room on one side and two bedrooms on the other.

Picture a 4-square court and then cram a bathroom and closet in the middle and you get the idea. But Mom and Dad love it.

(125 Loden Place)

HIGH SCHOOL SWEETHEARTS

Dennis and Sharon Bomgaars, my parents, dated in high school and married just a month after they both turned nineteen. Two days after their wedding, they moved from northwest Iowa to

Shreveport, Louisiana, where Dad was stationed with the United States Air Force. They were raised in Christian homes, but their faith came alive in Shreveport through Bible studies with other people in the military. As Mom and Dad studied Scripture, they became convinced that God was calling them to live simply and give generously. They felt the weight of the verse in Matthew chapter 6 that says, "Do not lay up for yourselves treasures on earth, where moth and rust destroy and where thieves break in and steal. But lay up for yourselves treasures in heaven, where neither moth nor rust destroys and where thieves do not break in and steal. For where your treasure is, there your heart will be also." Mom gave up her dream of a big house full of Ethan Allen furniture. She also gave away most of her wedding presents to Sister Margaret's Catholic Charity. With Dad's blessing, she even pawned her diamond engagement ring. Everything that wasn't a necessity was given away or sold as they broke with convention and followed their conviction that an uncluttered life filled with faith, family, generosity, and simple joys was the path God was leading them down.

After Dad left active duty military service, they moved to Jackson, Mississippi, so Dad could go to seminary. By this time Micah and Joel had joined the family and Dad was taking classes by day and working nights. He rotated through roles as a desk clerk at the Bill-Will Motel, a janitor at Stuart C. Irby Electric Company, and a security guard at the Mississippi Museum of Art. Mom was living her dream of being a stay-at-home wife and mother. Money was very tight, so when Mom got pregnant again, she called the hospital to figure out how much having a baby there would cost. It was expensive and they didn't have insurance, so she called a midwife and decided to have a home birth. Daniel was born in our little white house on the campus of the seminary, and it went so well she did it again when I came along 22 months later. But this time she gave birth to a 10-pound 2-ounce small toddler with no anesthesia after a long, hard labor. She did put in another call to the hospital, but this time it was to price having her tubes tied. Four kids under the age of five was a full cup for her, and there were no more babies after me.

THE BARN

Even though I'm 9 now, her hands are still full. She homeschools us kids and we're also our church's janitors. We started that job 3 years ago, so I've been earning my own money since I was 6. Mom and Dad are big on hard work and responsibility. That's how The Barn became the coolest clubhouse in Jackson.

Building clubhouses in the woods out of old lumber and cardboard was a regular pastime of both the Big Kids and the Little Kids, but rain ruined everything. After Dad got permission from our landlord to use the loft, he and my brothers tarred leaks in the tin roof, covered holes in the wood floor, and went dumpster diving for carpet remnants and furniture.

The most ingenious part of the clubhouse, and the source of our fun tonight, was electricity. Dad and the boys dug a shallow trench and buried extension cords all the way from our house to The Barn. Now we can plug in lamps, a stereo, and fans. A barn in Mississippi with no air conditioning and a metal roof is also called an oven.

The extension cord gave us Little Kids the perfect opportunity to start wars with the Big Kids, who always got first dibs on The Barn. All we had to do was unplug it in the house and the barn went dead. In less than 5 seconds, everyone in the loft flew down the ladder to make us pay. I still can't catch my breath from the excitement! If the Big Kids were getting bored up there tonight when we pulled the plug, they might be up for a combined game of Cops & Robbers through the woods and across the parking lots of the two churches that sandwich our dead-end street. If they're not bored yet, there are still a few more hours left before everyone has to go home. Plenty of time to play the power cord prank again. I think this is what people mean when they talk about kids having the time of their lives.

The sounds filtering through the woods tell me that Daniel and one of the other Little Kids have been caught. As my heart rate slows, I realize my stomach is a little queasy. Mom made all the kids homemade donuts tonight, and the Little Kids just ate ours when the idea for the extension cord prank hit us. It might have been a good idea to wait 30 minutes after we ate, like Mom said, before running. Mom loves having lots of kids over to play, and homemade donuts are a big treat. Scooping them out of the hot oil, she lays them on paper grocery bags to soak up the extra oil. Why doesn't she put them on paper towels or napkins? Simple. We don't buy those. Washcloths and towels fill almost every role in our family that disposable napkins and paper towels fill for other families. My parents' conviction about simple living wasn't just a fad. It stuck, shaping everything about our life. Mom also loves the natural world. She reminds us often that it's a spectacular gift from God. She reads all the time, and when she learned how trash is damaging the earth, she decided it was part of her responsibility as a Christian to care for God's creation. She can't bear to buy disposable things if she can help it, and she reuses everything. An empty cereal bag and a clothespin is her version of a Ziploc bag. Empty yogurt containers become Tupperware for leftovers. We never use plastic grocery bags, always paper. Those then get reused as trash bags in the kitchen. We have to be careful never to throw anything wet in the trash, or it soaks through, weakens the bag, and we have a huge mess of trash to clean up. My parents don't do all of these things because we're destitute. Dad has a great education and the work ethic of an Olympic athlete. They choose these things out of their conviction that a simple, generous life that cares for God's world is the life God is still calling them to. The message I get from my parents at every turn is this: When conviction and convention are at odds, you follow conviction. Not just in theory either. In practice.

There are so many things we do differently from mainstream culture. I struggle with conflicted feelings about being so different from "regular" families. On the one hand, I covet the canopy bed in the JC Penney catalog with the pink flowered comforter set and a matching bed skirt. Sometimes I just want to fit in - eat name-brand cereal, use band-aids with cartoon characters on them, and order pizza. Our family doesn't listen to secular music; watch Power Rangers or Rugrats; and I'm not allowed to wear 2-piece bathing suits because Mom and Dad are strict about modesty. On the other hand, I'm proud that my family is independent and doesn't follow the crowd. I mean, we have a barn loft with electricity for a clubhouse that's basically the same size as our actual house. Different isn't always bad.

(The Barn)

As I come out of the woods and trot back to the house, convinced I'll be safe from retaliation by this point, I hear Mom and Dad's laughter. It's my favorite sound in the whole world. Sometimes I hear it when they're listening to us kids tell them about our day. Other times I hear it when they're making jokes and quoting The Andy Griffith Show to each other. Other times it floats along with the breeze as they lay on a blanket in the backyard stargazing. I don't know anyone who laughs together as much as my parents do, and it makes me feel safe deep down.

As I round the corner of the house I see everyone under the big ash tree, munching the last of the donuts as they retell the prank and the chase to Mom and Dad. But alongside their laughter is another sound I hear every day. Police sirens.

CHAPTER 2

CALL THE POLICE

Spread out on a wooden board on the living room floor, the butterfly puzzle I'm working on is halfway complete. Our small living room only has a few square feet of open space so I have to finish puzzles quickly or they get walked on and messed up. Tonight Mom is reading aloud to our family from Anne Lindbergh's writings. Reading aloud is one of Mom's top priorities. It ranks up there with our family Bible reading and prayer before bed each night. When we kids were small she read picture books like The Berenstain Bears. Now it's classics like Jane Eyre and David Copperfield. To keep my brothers engaged she's started throwing in thrillers like Alistair MacLean's Ice Station Zebra.

It's a mild night, just like the night a few weeks ago when all our homeschooled friends were over and we played the extension cord prank. Mom doesn't believe in waste, so the air conditioner is off and the windows are open instead. As she reads, we hear two cars pull into the neighbor's gravel driveway. Muffled voices filter through the screened windows. They sound angry, but that's nothing new. We used to have seminary students who rented the houses on either side of us, but as crime increased in our part of Jackson, no students wanted to live there anymore. Now we have a revolving door of neighbors who often get drunk, their loud arguments floating in our windows. A couple of years ago one of our neighbors got drunk and shot and killed a man at a bar.

One of the cars roars away from the neighbors' house, just before frantic knocking at our door interrupts Mom's reading. A man and woman are standing there, shaking. They've just been followed and robbed at gunpoint by two men, they say, not 25 feet from where I'm sitting in our living room. They don't have a phone so they came to our house to call the police. Mom tries to keep me from hearing all the details because she knows I already struggle with fears about my physical safety, but the woman is hysterical and I hear her say, "He said, 'Give me your wallet or I'll blow your f***ing head off.'"

We live on the west side of Jackson, and although Loden Place is in the city, our landlord owns acres of land. We romp in the woods and ride bikes all over the property, but we also hear gunshots and police sirens just about every day. I feel safe on the inside from the warmth of our family life, but I know we live in a dangerous area. What if someone followed us home? What if they were willing to kill my parents over a few dollars?

As the man and woman retell their experience, the police arrive and the couple walks back to their driveway to file the report. But I can't walk away from the impact of the experience.

THE AIR I BREATHED

It's 1992 and politicians are ramping up tough-on-crime tv advertisements at the same time the robbery happens. Sounds like a great idea to me! I can put two and two together even if I'm only 9 years old. I'm also pretty sure everyone I know is a Republican, and I assume that if you're a Christian you're also a Republican. Researching candidates and voting is about as politically involved as Mom and Dad are, but everything I see and hear tells me our community is conservative through and through.

Pretty much everyone I know is also a Christian, and Christian principles are central in our home. We pray before every meal, go to church twice on Sundays and every Wednesday evening, and every night before bed we gather as a family to read the Bible and pray. Somewhere along the way, I've picked up that the faith and politics of our broader community are pretty tightly wound together. Our homeschool curriculum often has pictures of crosses and American flags next to each other, so in my mind, the Christian politicians urging us to be tough on crime are doing the Lord's work. But someone else is doing the Lord's work too, and I'm not sure she totally agrees with them. Her name is Mrs. Horton.

CHAPTER 3

MRS. HORTON

Running down the hallway at church with a thick stack of green paper in my hand, I round the corner and see Joyce Horton standing in the doorway of a classroom. Her wavy white hair is perfectly set, and small glasses are attached to a chain around her neck and balanced on the end of her nose. "Hi Christina!" she says brightly. Her sweet southern drawl always adds a few syllables to my name. There are two things I know about Mrs. Horton. First, she has a trampoline at her house and I want a trampoline very badly. Two, she volunteers at a prison, teaching Bible studies to the women there. She has a unique presence about her - like peace and joy wound together. It baffles me that someone as kind and radiant as her would work in a prison. Prison is for people like the robbers who mugged my neighbors. Why go there?

On Sunday evenings, the church service is at 6:00, but Dad almost always has a committee meeting beforehand. Tonight I tagged along early so I could help Mrs. Horton during the hour before evening church. Mom makes sure I'm there to help even on the days I'd rather skip.

Other people at church help Mrs. Horton too. Every year the ladies make cakes for a Christmas party for the women in prison. At other times we collect donations and assemble care packages of toothpaste, deodorant, and soap. But today Mrs. Horton has a group of us kids working on the project I like the least - refurbishing used Christmas cards. We cut pieces of construction paper in just the right shape and glue them inside the cards, covering the handwritten messages. Now they're ready for the women in jail to write in and send to their children.

This is hard for me to understand. It has never occurred to me that people in prison have children, much less send them cards. But I'm glad someone appreciates this tedious work.

As I walk into the classroom, Mrs. Horton takes the stack of green paper out of my hand and thanks me. Each one of those 50 sheets has a Christmas wreath and a Bible verse printed in one corner, colored by me. We don't always have enough Christmas cards to refurbish, so sometimes Mrs. Horton prints off a holiday design and has us color them. Then the women can fold the paper into a card. This takes way more time than a couple kids can do for 45 minutes on a Sunday afternoon, so I take a stack home sometimes and work on them in the evening while Mom reads aloud to us. Sometimes I feel like I'm losing my mind, coloring the same picture over and over again.

I don't really enjoy the card projects, but I do enjoy Mrs. Horton. She doesn't fit into my clear-cut view of the world as she talks about the women in prison like they're her family. She even calls them "my girls" and tells us how much they miss their children and how hard it is for them to be separated at Christmas. Her care for people whose lives are obviously messed up is baffling to me, but I've seen echoes of it in my parents too.

PAYING ATTENTION

Regularly when our phone rings at home, a man named George's drunken voice is on the other end. I don't even know how Dad met George, what his last name is, or what he looks like, but Dad talks on the phone or meets him at the public library. This routine has gone on for years. George never stays sober, but Dad makes time to listen and encourage him anyway.

Then there's Miss Savannah. A couple of months ago she moved in next door with her newborn baby, Anna Jo. Mom is always cautious with our neighbors because there's a lot of turnover and their lives are often marked by alcohol, broken relationships, and instability. So when Miss Savannah asked her to watch Anna Jo while she went to work, Mom immediately said no. But to my complete shock and joy, she changed her mind a few days later! She knew Miss Savannah was going through some really hard things, and the extra income would be nice too. Mom could help for a while. Miss Savannah dropped Anna Jo off early in the morning and we kept her all day for $1.50 an hour until she got off work. I was in heaven. A baby to feed and cuddle was my dream! But Miss Savannah didn't always pay Mom, and sometimes she would be hours late to pick Anna Jo up. Mom got so frustrated but tried to hang in there and help anyway. Their rocky relationship ended when Miss Savannah moved out after a few months, and we never saw Anna Jo again.

I see Mom and Dad show care for people who are struggling, and Mrs. Horton takes it a step further by caring for criminals. But it seems to me the world is pretty much made up of good people and bad people. Good people make good decisions, and bad people make bad ones. The life you have is the life you choose. If those women hadn't broken the law, they'd never be in Mrs. Horton's Bible study. If Miss Savannah was more responsible, she wouldn't be living in chaos. If George would stop drinking, he wouldn't need my Dad. Mrs. Horton and Mom and Dad blur the edges of my black-and-white picture of the world sometimes. A little gray here and there. But I don't have much room for gray. I've gotten very good at winning praise by being responsible, respectful, and hardworking. I've earned my own money from our church janitor job for three years, after all. If I can figure out the path to approval and success at nine years old, so can everyone else. One day my husband will tell me I have an unfortunate gift for judgment. It developed early.

Over the next several years, while I'm busy checking boxes and proving my view of the world correct, I'm also closing in on March 15, 1999, when my life will come to a screeching halt. Literally.

CHAPTER 4

INVISIBLE WOUNDS

The train car sways and I put one hand on a nearby seat, shifting my feet to keep my balance as we rumble down the tracks. I hold a deck of playing cards in my other hand as I stand in the aisle waiting for a friend to come with me to the lounge car so we can play our favorite game, Spades.

Mt. Salus Christian School, where Dad works, takes a ski trip every year with their 8th grade students and alumni. Last year they had a student drop out at the last minute and invited me to go along since I was 14 and the right age for the trip, even though I'm homeschooled. What an opportunity, getting to do something "normal" kids do like take a class trip! I only knew one of the girls who was going but decided to take the plunge, having the time of my life. This year they considered me an alumni and I got to come again, paying for it with money from my new job at Auntie Anne's Pretzels in Metrocenter Mall. Our group of 18 middle and high school students and chaperones took Amtrak trains up to Canada, skied for several days, and now we're an hour south of Chicago. It's our last night of the trip as we head home toward Loden Place.

The coach class car we're in has an upper and lower floor, with two seats on each side of a narrow middle aisle. We boarded on the lower level and climbed the cramped staircase to our seats on the upper level. As I stand in the aisle waiting for my friend to come back upstairs, one of the boys starts doing impersonations. The lights of a town streak past the windows as I giggle. Suddenly a huge jolt throws me off my feet. At the same time, I hear a loud boom and the lights flicker. Did we hit a car? How tragic! Even in the next second, as I try to grab another seat for an anchor and those thoughts flash through my mind, it never occurs to me that our train will do anything other than shudder to a stop. But we haven't hit a car. Later I'll learn we've hit a tractor-trailer loaded with steel rods.

For the span of a breath, there's total silence as the shock of the impact hits everyone. Then the air fills with screaming passengers and scraping metal as our car jumps the tracks, throwing us around as it skids along. The lights go out and it's impossible to get a grip on anything because the car is shaking so violently. My equilibrium changes as I'm thrown on my back and see nothing but darkness out the opposite windows. No lights from the town means I'm seeing the sky. We're tipping over. For a moment I wonder if I'm dreaming. Trains don't wreck like this.

They hit things, but they don't fall over! Time seems to move in slow motion. I think about the people that are alive right now that probably won't be in 20 seconds. Am I one of them? Are we over water, about to drown? On a hill, about to roll? In the path of another train car about to crash into ours? Are my life goals of getting married, having children, and living happily ever after over? Will I still be alive in 1 more second? What about 1 more? Over and over I say to myself, I'm still alive. I'm still alive. I'm still alive.

Our train car slams onto hard ground and screeches to a stop. It's pitch black, with people sobbing all around me. I'm still alive. The deck of playing cards is still clenched in my hand. A friend is under me, luggage on top of me. As we struggle to stand up, I look to my right and see a far-off street light out one end of our car. We aren't attached to the train anymore. Knowing it's important not to panic in a crisis, I willed myself not to scream while the wreck was happening. But as soon as I get to my feet, my body goes into shock and I start crying and uncontrollably shaking. Everyone is terrified fire will break out and we'll be trapped inside the car before help can get to us. We have to get out now. Several of the high school boys in our group climb up the seats and open an emergency exit window that's now above us as our car lays on its side.

I'm standing right under the window they open, so I drop the playing cards and climb up the seats and out the window, onto what is now the top of the car. I'm the first person out. My eyes struggle to take in the wreckage in front of me. Train cars strewn about and the far end of our car smashed into another car, with fire and black smoke billowing up.

The wreck happened next to a steel factory, and the men working the night shift have already rushed outside after hearing the crash. They are our first responders. One of them is already crawling across the top of our car on his way to help the people trapped in the burning car. He tells us to get out quickly, diesel fuel is spreading through the grass. Still in shock, I sit on the car next to the open window where I climbed out and pull my knees under my chin. There's still snow on the ground in patches, and the cold March air seeps through my gray Air Force sweatshirt and stocking feet. My shoes are somewhere below.

A few seconds later I hear voices calling up from the ground. Several other steelworkers are down there, telling me to climb down the wheels. The only light is from the fire as I try to shut out what I'm doing - climbing down the greasy wheels of an overturned train car - and let the years of climbing the mimosa trees at Loden Place take over. Move hands, then feet. Keep a secure point of contact. As I reach the ground, one of the workers takes my arm and leads me through the wreckage and toward the factory. I keep my eyes on the ground, not wanting to see the worst of the wreck. I know people are likely dying, but all I can do is put one foot in front of the other and just keep walking. The rocks surrounding the track are sharp and covered in mangled metal. I pick my way across them, leaning on the worker so the rocks don't cut my feet as we try to get away from this disaster.

The scent of diesel fuel and the sound of sirens and people crying fill the air. We reach a ditch leading up to the parking lot of the steel plant, and the worker picks me up, carrying me through the marshy grass before collapsing on the other side. As I catch my breath and stand up, the worker is already gone, weaving back through the wreckage to help more people get out. I'm alive. I'm safe.

INVISIBLE WOUNDS

Because I'm the first one out of our train car, there's no one else from our group to tell me what to do or where to go. No adults to give a hug or a plan. A trailer like you might see at a construction site sits next to the main building of the factory, and someone tells me I should wait there. Walking in, I see three pay phones. With no money to pay for the call, I dial the only collect number I can remember: 1-800-CALL-ATT. I have to try twice, my hands are shaking so badly that I misdial the first time. Mom answers my call. Still in shock, I blurt out that our train has crashed but I'm okay. On the other end, my parents envision the same thing that flashed through my mind during that first surreal moment of impact - a few wheels bumped off the track. Since we don't have cable tv at home, Mom and Dad only see how bad it is when images hit the internet later. It will be the second-worst wreck in Amtrak history.

Other people are lining up to use the phones, so I quickly hang up and turn around as a woman comes into the trailer. She breathlessly asks if anyone has seen two little girls named Rainey and Lacey. No, I haven't.

As I walk out of the trailer after calling Mom and Dad, I begin to see others from our group. After several hours we're taken to a local Farm & Fleet store that serves as a gathering place for train passengers. It's close to midnight now. Walking in, I see my friend who I'd been waiting on so we could play cards before this nightmare began, and run to give her a hug. This is the first time I knew that everyone in our school group is alive, though some do have serious injuries. After going to the hospital for X-rays of my ribs, we end up at the Lee's Inn hotel near dawn.

My two roommates fall asleep watching news coverage of the wreck. There's now one confirmed fatality. My stomach churns.

When I turn the tv off a few minutes later, the faint light of sunrise comes through the hotel window. Walking over, I stare out across open Illinois fields and watch that sky bloom in a spectacular array of purple, orange, pink, and blue. The colors blur as tears fall. Some of the people on our train won't get to see another sunrise. Instead, their families are waking up this morning to their worst nightmare.

INVISIBLE WOUNDS

In the months and years to come, I connect with several of the families who lost loved ones that night. I got a light snowfall of trauma from the wreck compared to the avalanche they received. The two little girls I was asked about as I called my parents in the trailer were young sisters, two of the eleven people who died. My parents still had their daughter. Matt and Cindy Lipscomb lost two of theirs. They were faithful Christians just like my parents, speaking on national news programs just days after the accident about their faith in a good God amidst unspeakable loss. Faith doesn't prevent suffering, and suffering isn't experienced equally.

What struck me even more, though, is the way trauma and grief are so often invisible on the outside. These families carry profound wounds that will not be healed in this world. But to walk past them on any particular day, you wouldn't know what they've been through. They still go to the grocery store, walk their dogs, and mow their lawns…even though their hearts are in pieces. Every time I heard about a tragedy after the wreck, I thought about these invisible wounds. In a world as broken as this one, people are getting mugged by life all the time. All around us, people are suffering. Grieving. Trauma and loss are part of our common experience as humans in a world that groans under the curse of sin and death. Our painful experiences may not leave wounds on our skin, but they always leave wounds on our souls. Sometimes the invisible wounds hurt the most and linger longest.

That cold March night as a 15-year-old, I experienced snowfall suffering. I was changed, but spared the worst. Six months later, my avalanche hit.

CHAPTER 5

UNTIL WE MEET AGAIN

Mom plans trips like other women plan their weddings. She pores over every detail, mapping out route options on the big Rand McNally atlas we have, scheming experiences on the cheap. It's been six months since the wreck, and Mom just got back from her first big trip alone, all the way out to Washington State to visit her brothers and sisters. It's my junior year of high school, and even though I'm homeschooled I didn't want to be gone for three weeks to go with her. This summer I hung up my Auntie Anne's apron and got two jobs as a waitress. I also just got my driver's license and bought my first car, a gray 1985

Pontiac 6000, for $1500. Life has returned to its regular routine, and there are friends to hang out with, money to be made, a car to drive, and boys to dream about.

(Me with my luggage from the wreck, in front of my "new" car)

As we lounge around the living room hearing stories from Mom's trip, she mentions that she's getting worried about her stomach. It's growing. She almost always wears loose dresses, and as she pulls her dress tight across her stomach, it's clear that something is wrong. It looks like she's pregnant.

After several doctor visits and scans, she gets the news that it's a massive tumor. My vibrant mother has stage three ovarian cancer. The doctors give her a 50% chance of living three years, even with surgery and chemotherapy. But as she and Dad do their own research, they can't find any studies where a woman with the specific type and stage of her cancer lived longer than 15 months.

MIRACLES

We prayed for a miracle, and we got one. She lived 3 more years. And live she did. A family member knew Mom loved to travel even though money was too tight to do it very often. They gave her several thousand dollars to take trips during the windows of health she had between surgeries and treatments, and I got to go with her on several of these adventures. The kindness and wisdom of this gift is something I will hold close to my heart until I die. We hiked through a rainforest in Washington State and splashed in the chilly waves along the breathtaking Oregon coast. We climbed a mountain in Colorado, singing at the top of our lungs to scare off any bears, and toured Prince Edward Island, the setting of the Anne of Green Gables books. Homeschooling gave me an unexpected gift here, allowing me to spend lots of time with the most influential person in my life during my last 2 years of high school.

As her health deteriorated during my sophomore year of college, Dad brought a hospital bed home to Loden Place so he could care for her himself, with the help of hospice nurses.

My precious mom passed away at home, during the night with Dad sitting by her side, on September 28, 2002. She was only 46.

Ever since she had children, Mom had struggled with a crippling fear that she would die before we were grown. Maybe it stemmed from her sister dying in a car accident when she was 17, or maybe Mom's own persistent health challenges of migraines, vertigo, ear infections, and vision problems kept her mortality always in mind. She wrestled with God almost daily for 2 decades, pleading for the privilege of raising her children. Her testimony as she neared death was that although God did not heal her on this earth, my brothers were living on their own and I was 19. He gave her the desire of her heart.

(Me and my mom, Sharon Bomgaars, just after she was diagnosed with cancer)

In many ways, the experience of the train wreck helped me through Mom's disease and death. I had seen firsthand how other people suffered. Losing a loved one was often part of life in a world torn apart by brokenness at every level. I was able to reconcile losing her, especially as I saw the many opportunities she had to share the eternal hope she had in Jesus even with a terminal diagnosis. But then the second wave hit.

Just 3 1/2 years after Mom died, Dad was diagnosed with lung cancer even though he never smoked. How could this happen? He was the picture of health. He walked me down the aisle at my wedding a year earlier. How could God let this happen? It felt like too much. A lot of people lose one parent, but the prospect of losing both felt profoundly unfair. There were lots of people who suffered a lot more than I did, but there were also people who suffered less. Couldn't one of them lose one parent instead of me losing both? Experiencing the unequal distribution of suffering now fell on me as it had on the Lipscombs who lost two daughters in the train wreck when I walked away with just scratches. Dad's diagnosis was even grimmer than Mom's. We were able to celebrate his 50th birthday between rounds of radiation, but my wonderful dad passed away on Christmas Eve 2006, just 8 months after his diagnosis. These two people, who gifted me with so much love and stability, and whose influence shaped every part of me, were both gone by the time I was 24.

(Me and my dad, Dennis Bomgaars, in the middle of his radiation treatments)

GRAY AREA

The painful experiences I'd been through by this point in my life had painted some warm tones of empathy into my clear-cut view of the world, but that empathy generally only applied to people whose suffering wasn't tied to their own choices. Being in the wrong place at the wrong time when a train crashed wasn't your fault. My parents getting cancer when they had been health nuts for years just seemed random. If your own choices led to your suffering, though, I still shrugged and stuck by my motto of "You reap what you sow." Empathy had been growing in me since the wreck, but it was conditional.

Over the next ten years, I leaned into my natural tendencies as a perfectionistic high achiever and felt I was reaping the rewards of making all the right choices. I had a happy marriage, wonderful sons, deep friendships, and was busy serving the Lord as a ministry leader at our church. My black-and-white picture of how life worked had expanded to include a large gray area of empathy for random suffering. The majority of the picture, though, was still rigid lines that removed question marks and gave me the predictability and certainty I craved.

When I reached to answer the phone on a bright December morning, a few months after my 32nd birthday, my ability to switch back and forth between empathy for the deserving and judgment for the undeserving, as I defined those categories, was so well-honed I couldn't even recognize it. It felt natural. And then, I received a surprise phone call…one that would change the trajectory of my life.

CHAPTER 6

THE CALL

"Christina, they have another baby, and I really think we're supposed to say yes." Time slows down as I take in what my husband, Thomas, is saying. Bundled up in my purple Columbia jacket that's a staple on our daily walks, I'm watching our 7 and 5-year-old sons, Cole and Tyson, ride their bikes down our street. Our 18-month-old, Brandon, is riding in the little blue car he loves, with the long handle attached to the back so I can push him.

Phone calls have been turning my life upside down for better or worse for a while now. It was a phone call that let me know Mom's tumor was cancerous. Another phone call letting me know I qualified for top scholarships, making the Christian university I wanted to attend financially possible. A phone call when my husband asked me out on our first date when I was a junior in college, and another phone call telling me Dad had a tumor. Sometimes phone calls have brought me great blessings, and other times excruciating pain. It's amazing how something as everyday as a phone call can shift the flow of your life in an entirely new direction.

As I hold the phone to my ear and listen to my husband talk, I can't believe what he's saying. Is he really asking me to bring another child into our home? No. I can't do it. I'm homeschooling our older boys, leading a foster care ministry at church, and trying to survive a very strong-willed toddler. Brandon is the first child we fostered, coming to us just a few weeks after he was born. We've been asked to take more kids since then, but Thomas knows it's out of the question. We both can see my hands are full. I thought we had agreed - our hands are still full! But that's the thing about calls. You don't decide when you get them or what they're about. You only decide if you'll answer.

THE PATH TO FOSTER CARE

Thomas and I met at Belhaven University in 2001; I was studying for a degree in Bible and he was pursuing Elementary Education. He was my first boyfriend, and we dated for a year before getting married over spring break of my senior year. One evening during our first year of marriage, I mentioned that I'd like to adopt a child one day. "Yeah, I would too," Thomas agreed. I grew up to love, value, and hold children in high regard. Mom and Dad taught me to value every life "from womb to tomb," long before the phrase was coined. They modeled it too as beloved children's teachers at church. I had also experienced enough personal loss by this time that I wanted to bring wholeness where there was pain. But that comment was the end of the conversation for years. Cole, our first son, was born when I was 25, with our second one, Tyson, coming two years later. We didn't want big gaps in the ages of our kids, so when Tyson was two we talked about adoption again. Never once did we talk about being a foster family. The thought of a child's parents living 10 minutes away sounded complicated and unnerving. In my mind, if we adopted a child from far away, they could leave all the bad experiences behind and have a fresh start. But we felt no direction for adoption. What country? What age? We didn't want to just pick something out of thin air. This was a living person we were talking about. As we were trying to figure out what path to take, a friend mentioned foster care. Even though we'd never even breathed that option out loud before, we both began to feel drawn toward it. Maybe we would foster for a couple of years while we figured out a path for adoption. Maybe the children we fostered would eventually need an adoptive home. It still sounded scary, but we began to feel a conviction that this was the path God had for us. We plunged in.

MORE THAN MEETS THE EYE

During the year Thomas and I were waiting to be approved as foster parents, another foster mom told me there was a conference called Empowered to Connect and we absolutely must attend. There are few things that stress me out more than not being prepared for something, so I got Thomas on board and we drove four hours to Birmingham, Alabama, for the weekend.

Over two days, the brilliant Dr. Karyn Purvis ushered us into the painful world of abuse and neglect and the impact it has on how children understand the world and themselves. It was the first time I heard about Adverse Childhood Experiences - a fancy term for childhood trauma - and the way they can impact mental, social, physical, and emotional health for decades to come. She helped us develop a compassionate imagination so we could see that the challenging external behaviors children from hard places often struggle with are a result of internal wounds. She shifted our focus away from the behaviors and toward what was causing them. If we wanted external behaviors to change, we had to focus on healing the internal wounds through helping children build trust, feel safe, and develop emotional connection. Empowered to Connect opened up the world of trauma and healing for me. It gave me "hooks to hang things on," which was Mom's way of visualizing the foundational knowledge you need in order to understand the next level of an idea. Electricians have to understand circuits. Business owners need to understand profit and loss. Pianists have to learn how to read music. And now I saw how crucial it is for foster parents to understand the impact of harm and the pathway to healing.

Now I have another opportunity to help a baby who is in a vulnerable situation. But as I pin my cell phone between my ear and shoulder and zip my jacket against the December chill, it just feels like too much.

I try not to shut Thomas down too quickly after he tells me about the new baby, stalling by asking for more details. In typical fashion, he didn't ask the social worker any questions, and he only knows two things - it's a baby, and he has a strong sense that God is asking us to say yes. He doesn't often sense that God is leading one way or another in our lives, so when he does I pay attention.

But I'm also a very practical person, and it seems to me that the person who does most of the child-rearing really ought to decide, and that's me! I'm not feeling the calling. In an attempt to be a team player, I agree to at least call the social worker and get the details. When I do, I learn that the baby is a newborn boy who is being discharged from the hospital after several weeks in the NICU. His mom used drugs while she was pregnant, and a judge ruled that the baby be removed from her custody until she proved that she could care for him. When I ask the social worker if she has other families who can take him if we can't, she says, "Well...no...I'll just have to keep looking." Drat. When would this baby be needing a foster family? I ask. "This afternoon," she replies. Drat again!

This is one ball too many in my frenzied juggling of life. But I also notice something. It's early December, a time when I'm usually addressing Christmas cards, agonizing over Christmas shopping, making treats for the 21 other houses on our street, and finishing our yearly family photo album that the kids unwrap on Christmas morning. Every year I commit to finishing all the Christmas preparations by Thanksgiving, vainly hoping to enjoy a stress-free holiday season. Thomas and I have been married for 10 years, and this is the first year that my plan to get it done early has actually happened. I even told him a few days ago that I couldn't understand it, but everything had fallen into place this year and my preparations were done!

As I watch our sons, now playing baseball in the front yard, I begin to sense what Thomas senses. Maybe God is asking us to say yes. Maybe God gave me an extra push to get prepared for Christmas so we could receive an unexpected gift. Within the hour we agree to take the baby. His name is Beckham, and this 5-pound 9-ounce treasure arrives on our doorstep a few hours later. I don't realize it yet, but this phone call just fused my life with the life of his mother - a woman who will open another new world to me, reshape my heart, and change my mind.

(Our family at the zoo 2 weeks before we got the call)

CHAPTER 7

FACE TO FACE

Our minivan crunches over the gravel as I pull into the child welfare office parking lot. The painted parking lines are long since gone, so I use a few other cars as a parking guide. Cole and Tyson unbuckle themselves and Brandon, and I hop out and unbuckle Beckham's infant seat. Slinging it over my arm as I turn around, I see a woman sprinting toward me. She's wearing jeans and a sweatshirt, but the first thing I notice are the tears streaming down her face. As she runs toward us, she never takes her eyes off Beckham. As she gets closer, I hear her talking, but it's not to me. She's talking to Beckham and as she reaches us she leans down and covers him with kisses and coos. In a bit of shock, I shift Beckham's car seat on my arm and smile a little too wide. It's my go-to move when I'm nervous, and I'm beyond nervous as she whispers to Beckham how much she loves him and how much she has missed him.

This is my first time meeting Joanne, Beckham's mom, and I have no idea what to do. This whole-hearted, vulnerable affection and emotion is not at all what I was expecting. Isn't this the same woman who used drugs while she was pregnant? How can a mom who would do that also love her child this much? I don't know much about addiction, but I have some experience with motherhood, and I have no category for this. The unsettled feeling I have now reminds me of the first day Beckham was with us.

When Beckham was released from the hospital after his birth and the social worker brought him to us, she stayed at our house for a few minutes as we got him settled. As we chatted, she made an offhand comment that it was like a funeral when she left the hospital with him. Joanne and the NICU nurses were all crying together. Wait, what? I couldn't understand that response from medical providers. Why weren't they condemning her for her prenatal drug use? Why weren't they relieved that he would be protected from her addiction? And why was she crying, when she made the choice to use drugs while she was pregnant? You reap what you sow. As I held Beckham for the first time that day and the social worker told me the story of leaving the hospital, she handed me a soft rag bunny. Joanne had been sleeping with it while Beckham was in the NICU, and she wanted me to put it next to him when he slept so he could still smell his mom even though she wasn't there. My confusion deepened. This was something a mother who understands the importance of bonding would think of, not a mother addicted to drugs. It reminded me of when my older boys were born and

I asked for the hospital to keep them in my room as much as possible so we could bond.

Fostering, even on the best days, is an emotional gauntlet of unknowns. Every time the phone rings it could be a social worker giving you life-altering information about a child's case. I didn't have the capacity for any more question marks in my life, so I focused on this adorable new baby and tried to push this sense of unease aside. But here it was again as I watched Joanne reunite with her son for their first visit.

I hold Brandon on my hip as Joanne takes Beckham's car seat and we walk up the concrete stairs into the child welfare office so she can start her one-hour visit with him. She can't stop talking about him and thanking me for taking such good care of him. The visitation room is tiny, with a worn couch spanning the length of one wall and a round table and chairs filling the rest of the space. After showing her the bottle I brought along so she can feed Beckham, I take my boys to a park down the road so she can have some privacy. When we return an hour later, I walk in the visitation room and see an image I'll never forget. Joanne is nestled in the corner of the couch, eyes closed, as Beckham sleeps on her shoulder. She's not asleep, and she's not scrolling on her phone. She's just drinking him in. The too-wide smile from nerves is back on my face as I say goodbye to Joanne and buckle Beckham's car seat back in my van for the ride home.

My brain is on fire. It's easy to see Beckham's life as precious and valuable. He's an innocent baby. I grew up going to pro-life vigils and prayer walks. I held compassionate pro-life signs by the highway at the yearly Life Chain event. I called elderly women in our church to get pledges for each mile I walked in the Walk For Life. I wasn't forced to do these things. Usually, Mom and Dad didn't even participate, but I asked if I could go with a friend whose family was active in the pro-life movement. The sanctity of human life was a personal passion of mine from a young age. Why was I feeling such strong resistance to seeing Joanne through the same lens of compassion, value, and worth as I saw her son? Was it because Beckham hadn't made any bad decisions yet, but she had? Of course, the sacredness of a person's life doesn't end when they make mistakes. It's just a lot easier to celebrate the image of God in an innocent baby than it is in adults after our broken world and choices get in the mix. Or was it because I grew up believing that bad people use drugs and really bad people become addicted? I knew foster care would bring me into some complicated situations, which is exactly why I wanted to avoid it. I need a nap.

(Joanne and Beckham at the hospital, just before the social worker took him away and brought him to our house)

The social worker told me early on that Joanne's #1 priority was getting into an addiction treatment center that also housed their client's children. The onsite nursery cared for the kids while the parents went to therapy and classes. Outside those times, moms and kids were together. I didn't even know that existed, and frankly, it sounded like a terrible idea to me. How could that possibly be a healthy environment for children? But there are two programs like that in Mississippi and one of them has a spot for Joanne. However, the judge presiding over Beckham's custody case wants him to stay with us for a couple more weeks until all of his medical appointments are complete. So Beckham stays with us while his mom starts in-patient treatment several hours away.

ACROSS THE MILES

Thomas and I agree Joanne can call me each day to get an update on Beckham while she's in treatment, and she never misses a day. This afternoon I have Beckham bundled up in his car seat on the kitchen floor as I'm wrangling the other three boys to get everyone out the door for a trip to the doctor. Joanne calls, and I answer even in the middle of the chaos because this daily phone call is a special privilege the treatment center is allowing her. She asks me how he's doing, how much he's eating, and any other tidbits I can share about the boring life of a newborn. Each bit of information is like a nugget of gold to her. Then she asks me to put her on speakerphone and hold the phone close to him. As I pause and do this, she sings "Jesus Loves Me" to him over the phone.

This intimate moment of mothering from miles away feels like holy ground. It's a raw, vulnerable display of affection—her taking the only chance she has for connection with him and pouring herself into it…while a stranger listens in. The next day she calls me when I'm pulling out of the driveway on another errand, and she has the same request. Please put her on speakerphone. The familiar melodies of bedtime songs fill the van. I have a front-row seat to Joanne's ocean of love for her son, and I feel it slowly unraveling me. Challenging me. Maybe I've misunderstood her. Maybe she's different from the average person who uses drugs. Part of me wants to unleash the compassion bubbling in my soul, but another part wants to avoid the stress of recategorizing her in my mind. Empathy uncovers complexity, and I don't need any more of that in my life. Besides, before I know it it's time to say goodbye and bring Beckham to join Joanne.

CHAPTER 8

GOING HOME

Beckham is sleeping in his car seat behind me as I drive through the flat farmland of the Mississippi Delta. The judge gave permission for him to join Joanne at the treatment center, and I volunteered to bring him there. He's only been with us for a month, but it feels like much longer. The quiet country roads and endless brown fields give me time to think. Like most foster parents, my brain struggles to know what path is best for Beckham...reunification with his mom or our home? The unknown versus the known divides my heart and makes what I am about to do extra difficult.

On the horizon, buildings the same color as the fields creep toward us. As we get closer I see high fences, razor wire, and skinny dark slots where windows must be. It's a sprawling prison complex, not something I'm used to seeing. Just looking at this one is unnerving. Maybe that's where my neighbor who killed a man is, or people like the men who robbed my other neighbors. I guess it makes sense that prisons aren't in high-traffic areas. These aren't exactly thoughts I want to dwell on. Out of sight, out of mind.

A few miles further we pull into the gravel parking lot of Fairland Center, where Joanne is in treatment, and walk into what feels like a surprise birthday party. Joanne scoops Beckham up and cuddles him close, radiating with joy. The staff at the center are exclaiming over how handsome he is and how proud they are of Joanne's journey to reunite with him. Several beautiful dogs used for pet therapy are happily weaving through the crowd. Over and over people come up and thank me for taking care of Beckham and supporting Joanne on her journey.

I've never been in an addiction treatment center, but this is not at all what I expected. It's impossible to tell the difference between staff and clients because both are dressed in casual clothes. The feeling of equality and camaraderie is so strong it almost feels like a family. The familiar feeling of uncertainty rages in me again, just like it did when the social worker told me it felt like a funeral when she took Beckham from Joanne after his birth. Where is the stigma? Where is the appropriate finger-wagging for the bad behavior of the clients that landed them here? Where is the hierarchy of respectable people who work here and suspicious people who need their help? This makes no sense.

Joanne and the staff want to give me a tour, so they show me her room. She has pictures I sent her of Beckham taped to the wall. Across the hall is the nursery where Beckham will be cared for while Joanne is in therapy and classes. We eat a meal in the dining room while one of Joanne's therapists introduces herself and shares some of her own story of recovery from addiction. She doesn't have an air of superiority over Joanne, and she doesn't treat me as though I'm Joanne's savior. We're all equals.

While everyone was genuinely celebrating Beckham's arrival, the receptionist quietly asked me not to take Beckham's things to Joanne's room. They'll need to be searched first to make sure nothing is coming into the facility that shouldn't be. Everywhere I turn I see that Fairland has managed to combine professional standards with a culture of warmth and equality. Not just for Joanne, but for everyone.

The tour continues as we walk out the back door to the gazebo and yard behind the center. Tears involuntarily slide down my cheeks. I can't stop myself from crying and I don't even know why. Someone gives me a hug. They think I'm struggling with grief over leaving Beckham, but I'm not. I'm truly happy for this little family to be reunited. I just can't process the experience of the last month. From the day we got the phone call about Beckham to this moment of celebration at the treatment center, my assumptions about drugs, addiction, and treatment have been challenged. It's really hard to rethink one thing, much less a whole bunch of things.

Every experience I've had with Joanne has been whispering to my soul, "She's a mom like you." I couldn't believe that in the beginning. No, she did things I would never do. But the more I've gotten to know her, and the more I see her love for Beckham, I've slowly been able to see the truth. I still don't understand her addiction and why its power wasn't broken when she got pregnant with a baby she desperately wanted and loved. But I see now that Joanne is a mom like me who loves her son just as much as I love my three sons.

Unlocking that door in my heart and letting her occupy a place as an equal has been emotionally exhausting, and I'm feeling relieved that the journey is almost over. But here I am at a treatment center that seems to operate on the belief that Joanne is not unique. She's not the one "good addict" in a thousand bad ones. She is simply a regular person struggling with a complex health crisis who needs healing, not shaming. She isn't any different from the next person inside the clinic...or outside of it. Needless to say, this message challenged my "bad people use drugs and really bad people become addicted" perception that remained tucked inside me ever since I was a little girl...and I wasn't ready for it.

I didn't sign up to be a foster parent because I wanted to rethink anything. Solving problems was my goal, not discovering question marks. But once I started seeing, I couldn't unsee. And I didn't want to unsee, really. There was something happening that gave me an odd sense of hope, and I could feel a shift inside from suspicion to curiosity. All my life I'd been taught that fear is the right response to drugs. But I knew from the Empowered to Connect foster parent conference that fear shuts down our ability to think and reason. If I was going to learn, I needed to lay down fear and get curious.

Was Joanne a unicorn, or had I radically misunderstood addiction? Could there be better ways to value the sanctity of life and the image of God in people who are struggling with it? Would a different response to addiction produce better outcomes than the shaming, blaming one we've tried for so many years? I didn't have answers yet. But all I could keep thinking was, "Almost every American family is impacted by drugs and addiction. If there is a better solution, the impact would be breathtaking! I have to know."

PART II: LEARNING JOURNEY

CHAPTER 9

RAT PARK

My heart jumps as I see who the email is from. I didn't expect to hear back from Dr. Alexander at all, but less than 24 hours later I have a reply from him. It's been 18 months since I brought Beckham back to Joanne. She graduated from treatment and is sober and thriving as a mother with a full-time job. Three days after Beckham left our home we got a call from another social worker who had another newborn needing a foster family, and Jonas has been with us since then. Now we have 8-year-old Cole, 6-year-old Tyson, 3-year-old Brandon, and Jonas. Homeschooling, potty training, and nap schedules fill my days, but over the last 18 months, I've also been on a journey of learning. The questions churning through my mind that day at the treatment center didn't go away, and I've been reading research and listening to personal stories as I've looked for answers. One of the people who has helped me the most is Dr. Bruce Alexander.

I came across his work on addiction in the book *Chasing the Scream: The First and Last Days of the War on Drugs*, by Johann Hari. That book, with its combination of fascinating research and gripping storytelling, has been the most helpful resource on my learning journey. Dr. Alexander's work, highlighted in *Chasing the Scream*, connected so many dots for me that I sent him an email about it. Since he has traveled the world speaking on drug use and addiction as a psychologist who has studied it for over 50 years, and I'm a random stay-at-home mom from Mississippi, I assumed he would be too busy to respond. Now I'm staring at his thoughtful reply in my inbox! Turns out, it would be one of several I'd receive over the course of the coming years.

Dr. Alexander grew up in an earlier generation than I did, but experienced the same messaging I did about people who struggle with addiction. Because of what he thought he knew, he was quite nervous when he was assigned to work at a clinic providing medical care for those very people. A young psychologist in the 1970s, he explained why. *"I was afraid, you know, because I had learned that these people were terrible cunning liars and thieves."* As he worked at the clinic, he started seeing something unexpected. The people he was treating had problems he could easily understand, and they actually wanted to tell him their stories…true stories. That is, as long as he would listen without spouting his academic theories at them.

Alongside his work at the clinic, Dr. Alexander was also teaching at a university in Vancouver, British Columbia, Canada.

He began sharing with his university students what he was learning from his clients about the reasons they were using drugs. He was becoming convinced that it wasn't because they were morally bankrupt people. It was because they were hurting in some way, and drugs and the camaraderie they developed with other drug users allowed them to numb those painful feelings. Half of his students found his patients' experiences interesting, and the other half, he remembers, told him, "Don't believe them, they're lying!" The students who scoffed at the idea that addiction was caused by anything other than the power of a drug based their belief on a 1960's experiment that was somewhat recent at the time.

In the experiment, a rat is put in a Skinner box. These small boxes allow researchers to study how an isolated animal's behavior is altered by rewards like a food pellet or punishments like an electric shock. The rats in this experiment were put in empty Skinner boxes with a lever on the wall that the rats could easily press. Pressing the lever injected a little heroin or cocaine into the rat, through a tube that was connected to an artery in the rat's circulatory system. The rats often pressed the lever, sometimes so frequently that they overdosed and died. The message that came out of those experiments, Dr. Alexander recalls, was, "This is what these things do to you. You start using them and you just do more and more and more and more until you die. Stay away from these drugs."

The rat experiment was seen as proof of what was widely believed at the time: There are certain drugs that are so powerful that if you try them once you'll be hooked forever. Or at least until they kill you.

As Dr. Alexander learned about the rat experiments, though, he had a nagging sense that something was wrong. It didn't match up with what he knew about rats. Rats are highly social creatures, like humans. They love to play, explore, and socialize. Yet Skinner boxes are empty. There's nothing to play with or explore, and no one to socialize with. It goes against their nature and needs. Being stuck in an empty cage for a rat is like being stuck in solitary confinement for a human.

So Dr. Alexander and several colleagues decided to do their own experiment. They kept the lever for the rats to get drugs anytime they wanted, but they put the rats in a different environment built on the floor of their laboratory: Rat Park. It had sawdust for the rats to roll around in, tin cans to hide in, plenty of room, and plenty of rat friends. It was everything a rat could want in life. They studied the rats in this environment. Even though the rats could push the lever to get drugs any time they wanted to, they rarely did. In Rat Park, they preferred to be sober. Even when they pushed the lever and got drugs, they never used in excess.

Dr. Alexander concluded that rats' drug use wasn't driven by the drug. It was driven by their environment. When they were happy and had their needs met, they didn't want the drugs. When they were stripped of everything that makes a rat happy, they used drugs excessively. This discovery opened a world of possibility.

"Could this also be true of humans?" Dr. Alexander wondered. Could a person's circumstances and experiences have far more influence than the drug itself on whether he or she became addicted?

His results with the rats in Rat Park fit with what he was learning at the clinic from real people struggling with addiction. It was their suffering, not the drug, that led them into addiction. It was what they didn't have access to that influenced their choice...not what they did have access to.

In some small way, I feel like I can relate to this idea that behavior often has deep roots and that our experiences echo in our lives for years to come. After my neighbors were robbed when I was 9, I developed severe anxiety about safety. Every time we drove somewhere in the evening, I watched out the back of our red station wagon. Dread filled my heart when a car was behind us. If it turned when we did, my heart raced and my stomach flip-flopped. When the car turned onto another road, relief washed over me. They weren't following us. Driving at night became terrifying for me. Desperate to feel safe, I even begged my parents to move out of Mississippi. That anxiety over physical safety did lessen over the years, but it never went entirely away.

After 30 years, I still lock my doors at home, even during the day. I'm not sure there's ever been an armed robbery in the gated neighborhood where my family and I live. But the experiences of our childhoods are like chain reactions, echoing decades into the future as they shape our thoughts and behaviors. What happened when I was 9 still impacts me at 39.

The train wreck has similar echoes. I don't prefer to fly because my body still overreacts to sensations that are similar to the wreck. Being in rows of seats with an aisle up the middle during jolts of turbulence triggers clammy hands and a racing heart. Even something as mundane as hitting a big pothole in my van can trigger that same reaction.

Trauma lingers, and grief does too. When I hear a friend say, "My mom called me today," a little current of pain runs through my heart. I'm thankful they can say those words, but I'll never get to say them again.

If my own experiences still whisper in my ear decades after those events, surely the same is true for other people. Exponentially more so for people who have experienced abuse or neglect. Our behaviors today don't exist in a vacuum. The pain we experience has a way of seeping into the deepest parts of us and lingering.

As I learned about Rat Park, I was also diving deeper into the research on Adverse Childhood Experiences (ACEs). First learning about them at the Empowered to Connect conference, they resurfaced as I learned about addiction. The connection between ACEs and the risk of addiction was inescapable. The more ACEs a person has, the higher his or her risk of addiction.[1] Rat Park was making more and more sense. If people struggle with addiction, it doesn't mean they are bad. It means they are hurting. Just like the people at Fairland Center first showed me when I dropped Beckham off with Joanne. On a much smaller scale, maybe addiction is a little like fever. Fevers aren't a sickness. They are our body's response to sickness, indicating something else is wrong. Addiction is an indicator that something deeper is very wrong. It could develop as a response to abuse, neglect, anxiety, depression, mental health challenges, disconnection, guilt, loss, isolation - any number of painful experiences.

The more I thought about it, the more it made sense why people whose addictions have taken the most from them often seem to have the hardest time finding recovery. Suffering isn't distributed equally. The deepest addictions are often the result of the deepest suffering.

Inflicting blame, shame, and pain has always been a futile way to stop addiction. Now we know why.

PAYTON

When I met a man named Payton, this new lens of looking beneath the surface of addiction let me see in living color what I previously only saw in black and white.

Payton grew up in a suburb of Jackson, MS, about 20 minutes from me. He lived with his mom after his parents divorced, though he was often home alone while she worked two jobs. When he was 13, his mom quietly came into his bedroom early one morning, kissed him, and whispered goodbye. Payton pretended to be asleep, but after she walked out of his room and closed the door, he watched out the window as she pulled away from the curb with a U-Haul trailer. He thought she was working so much to provide for him. Now he realized she had been saving up to leave. Even though Payton had a great relationship with his dad and moved back in with him immediately, the experience of his mom's abandonment changed him. Trauma lingers.

Some of Payton's friends started dabbling in marijuana around this time, but Payton stayed away from it, perfecting tricks on his skateboard instead. He struggled in other ways, though. It became nearly impossible for him to focus on his schoolwork after his mom left. He held it together for a few years, but at 17 he dropped out of high school and began using marijuana and alcohol. It made him feel better, numbing those hidden wounds.

Payton did end up going to community college, studying to be a chef, and over the next 10 years he had incredible opportunities as well as painful endings. Those endings, with the acute sting of rejection that echoed the rejection he felt as a 13-year-old when his mom left, led to more drug use–this time it included opioids. "I think I just kept taking the pills because it could numb emotional pain," Payton explains. "It could numb rejection, loss, all of that, and could keep my body moving and doing whatever I needed to do to get through my shifts." His occasional use of opioids became daily use. A pill in the morning helped him get going. That turned into a pill in the morning and in the afternoon. Soon he was taking 2 pills in the morning, 2 in the afternoon, and 1 at night. The body builds tolerance to opioids over time, so Payton needed higher doses just to get high. The body also becomes physically dependent on opioids when a person uses them regularly, so now Payton was caught in a cycle of needing drugs to keep the emotional pain at bay as well as the physical symptoms of opioid withdrawal.

Before I read about Rat Park, I would've looked at Payton's life and assumed he was a particularly bad person because he dropped out of high school and started using drugs. I would have seen Payton as a 20-something chef addicted to opioids…a man easy for me to judge, shake my head, and wonder why he doesn't quit before he loses his job. Now I saw it through a very different lens as I looked under the addiction to the hidden pain fueling it. Now I could see Payton as the young boy trying to make sense of his parents' divorce. Payton the teenager watching his mom walk out on him. Payton the high school student feeling like a failure and dropping out because he struggled to focus as the trauma lingered. Payton the teenager finding something that numbs all that pain, even though it's costly. The new lens of Rat Park helps me see the hidden labyrinth of experiences and pain that drive the harmful behavior of a smart, talented, hard-working man.

It reminds me of an exhibit at the McWane Science Center in Birmingham, Alabama. There's a fake anthill about 8 feet off the ground, hanging over an open area. Below it is a mold, suspended in the air, of all the ant tunnels you can't normally see because they're underground. The tunnels start at the anthill and extend about 6 feet below the surface, sprawling outward in a web. It's an incredible exhibit, giving us a peek into something we never see otherwise - the vast, complex world beneath that visible mound of fire ants.

We regularly have fire ants set up shop in our yard. I hate those anthills, and when Thomas and I first bought our house I would pour boiling water on them in the hope that they would go away. The first time I see the sculpture at the science center, I smile. The visible part of an ant's home is only a very small part. What creates it is deep underneath, hidden from view. Maybe addiction is similar. We see the problem behavior - the anthill. But we miss what's underneath it - the deep, wide web of experiences and risk factors that lead to it. Maybe addressing what we don't see is the key to addressing what we do.

Dr. Alexander's Rat Park experiment was groundbreaking, but it contradicted the prevailing ideas of the day. The research was met with fierce resistance in the academic community. "That simple experiment turned out to be quite inflammatory news for a lot of people," Dr. Alexander remembers. "Some people were really mad. They didn't believe it and they didn't want to hear it." This made sense to me when I thought about my own resistance to the uncertainty Joanne brought into my life. Rethinking anything is hard. When you add the professional investment of careers built on the idea that the drug itself is the primary cause of addiction, the cost of rethinking goes up dramatically.

I ask Dr. Alexander why he thinks we tend to fall back on simple understandings of addiction. "To look at the full nature of the problem is quite demanding," he says. I couldn't agree more. Sometimes I just want to shut out what I'm learning and go back to "Bad People + Bad Drugs = Addiction." It may be an illusion, but it's a simple story. It's easy to demonize the drug and much harder to ask why people want to use it. The latter unlocks a world of complexity from hopelessness, trauma, loneliness, anxiety, depression, and mental health challenges. There is no simple solution, no matter how desperately we want one.

If it's true that drugs are an attempt at a solution and not the real problem, then no matter how chaotic, destructive, or messy an addiction is, it can only be healed by addressing the pain that's driving it. Addressing the drugs numbing that pain gets us little to nowhere.

As things begin to click and make sense in my mind, I can't help but wonder, "Is this what's going on with Joanne? Is this why her pregnancy with a baby she desperately wanted still wasn't enough to stop her from using drugs?" I knew what Dr. Alexander might say…

CHAPTER 10

BEHIND THE SCENES

Some of Joanne Shedd's earliest memories are of happy days when Miss Denise came to clean her family's Vicksburg, Mississippi, home. The different scents of her cleaning supplies filled the house, as did her love for Joanne. These happy days were interspersed with days when Joanne's dad took her with him to the house he was building for their family in Jackson. He showed Joanne, just a preschooler then, how to screw the electrical covers on the wall outlets, and she did her part to put the finishing touches on their new home.

Joanne is one of four children, just like me, and her parents also made the counter-cultural decision to homeschool back in the pioneering days of the homeschool movement. They went to church every time the doors were open, and Bible reading and prayer were a part of their family's daily rhythm too.

The same year Joanne moved to their new home in Jackson, a boy showed her attention for the first time. She was on the playground at preschool and Casey offered her one of his Cool Ranch Doritos. Joanne vividly remembers the moment, including the bag that advertised this new flavor. She felt so special, so validated. From that time forward, she chased this feeling.

Throughout her growing-up years, she worried about other people's opinions. Being homeschooled, she felt different from all the other kids who went to school, including most of the kids in her church youth group. She hadn't seen the movies, watched the tv shows, or listened to the music that other kids had. But she still craved validation, so she looked for other ways to find acceptance. Other than one or two friends who were also homeschooled, Joanne's social options came from church. The other girls in their vibrant youth group were "good girls," but Joanne was interested in some of the older guys in the youth group. The "bad boys." Although her parents were strict about who she hung out with, the boys came from good families in the church so they let Joanne spend time with them.

What her parents didn't know was that Boone's Farm citrus wine and marijuana became a regular part of their hangouts. This was Joanne's first experience with alcohol and marijuana, and she didn't like either one. But she drank and smoked anyway because it helped her fit in and feel accepted. Soon she started smoking cigarettes for the same reasons. Anything that was different from her straight-laced upbringing was intriguing to her.

People who lived on the edge and embraced freedom and risk seemed so cool.

A year later, when Joanne was 14, she started babysitting for a family who lived a few miles away. Walking into their house for the first time, Joanne smelled cigarette smoke. Wow, a family who smoked *inside* their house! That was definitely living on the edge. As she scanned the rest of the house, she saw lots of alcohol. She didn't drink any of it, but when the parents came back that night and gave her $40, their coolness factor shot through the roof. Before them, Joanne had been babysitting for all the homeschoolers who paid $2 an hour. Getting $40 for 5 hours was a windfall!

Over the next 2 years, this family's influence on Joanne's life would be monumental. It wasn't long before she was drinking their alcohol while she babysat. Not only were they ok with it, but they also encouraged her to. Soon marijuana and benzodiazepines entered the picture. It wasn't long before they stopped paying Joanne in cash and just let her have friends over to drink and use whatever drugs they had in the house.

During this time, Joanne's parents didn't know what was really going on there. She kept eye drops everywhere to combat the bloodshot eyes that came with getting high, and she often spent the night at the family's house so she was sober by the time she went home. Her mom had a lot of hesitations about the family and often told Joanne she felt like something wasn't right, but Joanne begged her mom to let her keep babysitting. She didn't mention that she was desperate to keep going over there because there were no rules and it was a wild party every time. As the couple's drug use took off, and Joanne's with theirs, the times she went to babysit weren't babysitting at all anymore.

The kids went to their grandparents' house and Joanne just went over to party.

By the time she was 16, Joanne was lying to her parents constantly to cover up the life she was living. Their relationship became very strained as her parents started to grasp just how much she was hiding from them. A new boyfriend entered Joanne's life, and even though their relationship was extremely unhealthy, he offered an escape from the tension at home. At 17 she moved out with him and later they married. For the next fifteen years, Joanne's drug use ebbed and flowed, filling in the cracks of a deeply unhappy life.

She doesn't look back on her childhood and see huge traumas, though. Joanne had a pretty happy childhood before her decisions as a teenager snowballed into many years of pain, drug use, and addiction. She sees a lot of little things that made her desperate to gain approval and validation. Pushing the boundaries felt good too. And as she pushed those boundaries and found validation in harmful ways, she was exposed to drugs as well as to a chaotic lifestyle and toxic relationships that very quickly gave her a lot of experiences she wanted to numb.

As I mull over Rat Park and the hidden causes of addiction, Joanne's story helps me understand the nuance and complexity of it all. Although many people, like Dr. Alexander's clients and like Payton, can trace the desire to numb to an abusive childhood or a traumatic event, not everyone can. There does always seem to be pain in the person's life, but addiction is far too complex an experience to be put in a clearly defined box with a bow on top.

Kevin Armstrong is a friend and therapist who has a private practice up the road from my house, but he also offers counseling for men at a jail nearby. In both places, he works with people who struggle with addiction. I ask him one day about his experience of the root causes of addiction given that not everyone who struggles had a traumatic childhood.

Kevin tells me that one of the men he works with who's in jail was abandoned on the streets when he was 8 years old. One of the men he counsels in his private practice grew up in a wonderful Christian family but was emotionally abandoned by his pastor father whose time was sucked up by all the other people vying for it. Their life experiences are radically different, "But both are struggling with feelings of abandonment," Kevin tells me. They both turned to drugs to cope with the pain. Kevin also mentions a term I haven't heard before - process addictions. They're not substances we ingest like heroin or cocaine, they're processes we do like gambling or watching pornography. The people Kevin works with struggle with relapse from process addictions just as much as they do with drug addictions. I consider this another point in favor of focusing less on the drug - the coping mechanism - and more on the pain that underlies it.

As I reflect on the very different childhoods and life experiences of Payton, Joanne, and Kevin's clients, it seems important to resist the urge to paint even my new understanding of addiction with too broad a brush. Dr. Alexander himself strongly cautions against this. We can learn about trends and risk factors without moving to extremes. He even refers to Rat Park as a springboard into a complicated issue, not the final word on it. Rather, it shifts our focus away from the drug as the main catalyst for addiction and invites us to get curious about the other factors in a person's life that make them susceptible. That's where we're most likely to gain traction toward preventing drug use in the first place and helping people who do struggle with addiction to overcome it.

Joanne's life was quickly accumulating more and more of those factors as abusive relationships and poor choices gave her even more experiences she wanted to numb. Like a snowball gaining size and momentum as it rolls down a mountain, the pain that started the addiction often grows into more pain through the addiction. Joanne lived this reality.

It makes me wonder how we could identify the early stages of addiction and protect people from additional pain so they can find a path to healing before the snowball gains so much speed it becomes nearly unstoppable. For Joanne, it would be nearly two decades before she found her path out.

At one point she lived in a house with a drug dealer who was robbed by armed gunmen while Joanne looked on in terror. At another point, she was so drunk when she showed up to her job as a restaurant server at Bravo! Italian restaurant in Jackson that she lay on the floor in the back while the owner served all of her customers. As the years blurred into each other, the dysfunction grew. Her marriage was a disaster, her friendships were temporary, and she was in a long spiral downward. There were people who hurt her, but she also hurt a lot of people, and she doesn't shy away from the role she played in the implosion of her life and marriage.

When she left her husband, after 10 years together, she tried a drug she hadn't liked as a teenager – crystal methamphetamine. Now she loved it. Too much. Methamphetamine is a stimulant, so when she took crystal meth she could stay up for days at a time before crashing in exhaustion. She started missing shifts at the restaurant and coming in late to work because of her meth use. Within 4 months she got fired from a job she'd held for 12 years. It would be 5 more years of the roller coaster of addiction and dysfunctional relationships before Joanne got the surprise of her life. She was pregnant.

She always wanted to be a mother, but doctors told her for years she would never be able to have children. Overjoyed at this new life growing inside of her, she knew something had to change with her addiction. But breaking a nearly 20-year cycle of drug use is no small task. Her pregnancy progressed, and she went for short periods of time without using but always relapsed. She held out hope that maybe she would be able to stay sober by the time he was born. But when she went into labor several weeks before her due date, that hope died. She knew Beckham wouldn't be coming home with her because she had methamphetamine in her system. Instead, her son was removed from her custody and a social worker brought him to me, starting a different kind of snowball rolling down the mountain. This was a snowball of curiosity, though. About the root causes of addiction, about what I'd misunderstood about harm and healing, and about how the story would end once Beckham went home.

CHAPTER 11

A FORK IN THE ROAD

Thomas, my husband, and I walk into Sal & Mookie's pizzeria with Cole and Tyson in tow. They're 8 and 6 now. We left Brandon and Jonas at home with a sitter so we could focus on the reason we came. Today is Beckham's 1-year-old birthday party, and Joanne invited us. We walk to the back of the restaurant where several tables are pushed together so everyone can fit. Joanne's family is there, as I expected. We met most of them while Beckham was with us, and there are hugs all around. This truly is a day of celebration. As I sit down, Beckham's social worker from his time in foster care sits across from me. One of the nurses who cared for Beckham in the NICU after he was born is sitting on my left. This isn't just a family celebration, it's a community celebration of the life, healing, and restoration we've all gotten to witness over the last year. As we catch up, one of Joanne's family members looks at me and says with wonder, "Can you believe we're here? Who would have thought this was possible?" She wasn't talking about this date fitting into everyone's schedules. She was taking in the monumental change in Joanne's life after years of watching the chaos unfold. Transformation happened. Not on anyone's preferred timeline, including Joanne's. Not without deep wounds for many of the people at that table. Not without herculean effort on Joanne's part to build a new life with new rhythms, habits, schedules, priorities, and coping mechanisms. But it happened, and we were allowed to witness it. To be part of it. And today, to celebrate it. Joanne radiates with joy as she holds her little man who looks adorable in tiny jeans and a button-up green plaid shirt.

One of my favorite stories from Joanne about this year of recovery happened while Beckham was still with us. She missed him so badly and wanted desperately to stay sober and regain custody, so she was participating in everything the treatment center offered, including having an ice cream sundae one Saturday afternoon. Chocolate syrup and caramel syrup sat next to the ice cream, and Joanne had always chosen chocolate because it's what everybody else liked. But as she stood by the table that day, she reached for the caramel. As she sat on a chair in the hallway outside her bedroom, Joanne ate her ice cream with caramel sauce and felt like she'd just discovered a secret. It was something about herself she'd never noticed before because she spent so many years just trying to fit in and do what other people wanted or like what they liked. She was beginning to know herself instead of numb herself.

As we sing happy birthday to Beckham, the memories of my Sunday afternoons with Mrs. Horton echo in the background. Milestones like this are what the women she cared for in prison were heartbroken to miss. When we drove past that prison complex on the way to bring Beckham home to her, I was reminded of just how many people are sitting in prison. She was using illegal drugs just a year ago, but she wasn't arrested and put in prison. She got to spend time in a treatment center that helped her heal. I can't help but feel uneasy wondering where we'd be today if she'd been given handcuffs instead. It wasn't long before I saw the answer to that question with my own eyes, through another young mother.

TURNING POINT

Walking into the courtroom just before 9:00am, I feel the tension in the air. I've never been in a courtroom for criminal cases before, but I'm here this morning supporting a woman who is being sentenced for behavior stemming from her own addiction. I sit on the hard wooden bench and glance around at the other people taking similar seats. I didn't realize the family and friends of everyone being sentenced this morning would arrive at the same time, nor did I realize we'll be watching the sentencing of other people as we wait for our loved one's turn. This is my first time in a criminal courtroom, and all I know is what I've seen on *Law & Order*. I assume there will be lengthy arguments from attorneys on both sides, with each case taking at least an hour or two before the judge reaches a decision. As cases are called, I realize why we all came at the same time. Case after case is decided in just 5 or 10 minutes. Some of them seem like formalities, with agreements reached behind closed doors that are simply being formalized here. Others have a prosecutor and defense attorney making their cases. Even for those, the speed is dizzying. It took me longer to feed the boys their breakfast this morning than it takes for most of these cases to be heard and a sentence handed down.

As each case is decided, some of the family and friends on the benches near me leave too, but my friend's case hasn't been called yet. Directly across the aisle from me is a very pregnant woman. As the next defendant is brought in, he scans the attendees, locks eyes with her, and mouths "I love you." He's wearing an orange jumpsuit and his wrists and ankles are shackled just like every other defendant even though some of them are facing minor charges. He shuffles to the defense table and takes a seat facing the judge. The prosecutor explains the non-violent drug charge the defendant is accused of and highlights that he had a prior drug charge. The defense attorney acknowledges the prior drug charge but notes it was more than a decade ago and connected to an addiction he has struggled with. He asks the judge to divert the defendant to drug treatment instead of sending him to prison.

The pregnant woman is allowed to speak last. Her floral maternity dress swishes as she approaches the podium and reads her appeal to the judge from loose papers clutched in shaking hands. Through tears and an occasional sob, she begs the judge to let her fiancé come home. She's due with their first child, a little girl, in less than a week. She wants their daughter to have a present father, and she knows the devastating impact of incarceration on children because her own father was incarcerated when she was growing up. "Please let him come home," she pleads to the judge. "He's a good man. We need him."

She walks back to her seat, wiping her tears. The judge was quiet while she sat down but immediately hands down the sentence. Sixteen years in prison. His gavel rings through the courtroom accompanied by anguished cries from the defendant and his fiancée. Next case. I can barely breathe. A family has just been torn to pieces in less than 15 minutes. How can a society that values families so much be willing to tear them apart like this for a minor infraction? Maybe I'm naive, but I never pictured this when I thought about our court systems in America.

The cases continue, but my mind pushes pause as I try to trace the ripple effect of what just happened.

For the man, he'll obviously lose his job. Without a job, you can't maintain housing. Is that where his fiancée lives too? Is he the breadwinner? Will she be left with no income or housing and a new baby? As someone who heard from my earliest days how important intact families are, I can't help but think how the last 15 minutes will affect the next 15 years. How can this man possibly maintain a relationship with his fiancee through so long of a separation? How can he develop a relationship with his daughter who will be old enough to drive before she ever spends one day with her dad? From research I've read, I know that having a parent incarcerated is an ACE (Adverse Childhood Experience). Putting this father in prison will echo through his daughter's life, amplifying her own experiences of trauma and loss, beginning the formation of her own snowball, and increasing her own risk of addiction before she even draws her first breath. These last fifteen minutes won't just affect the next 15 years, but the next 50.

The more I think about the future of this little family, the more it seems that incarceration is like tipping over the first domino of a domino run. It sets off a chain reaction of collateral damage to families and communities. And what about the defendant's addiction? Prison certainly won't stop him from using drugs. I've already heard from numerous people that drugs are easier to get in prison than they are in the free world. Will he be right back where he started 16 years from now? No, I don't think so. He'll have spent 16 years in an environment full of extreme physical, mental, and sexual trauma. He'll be unemployable with a felony on his record, and housing is hard to come by if you don't have income. Seems much more likely that prison will add even more size and momentum to the snowball of pain that I now realize drives addiction.

I can't get the thought of Rat Park out of my mind. If disconnection, isolation, and trauma are significant drivers of drug addiction, then isn't prison the worst possible response? It seems like the cycle of suffering that prison inflicts is basically a cycle of forced trauma. So we're using trauma to fix a problem that's made worse by trauma. No wonder we aren't getting more of the outcomes we want. We're pouring gasoline on a fire.

As I'm connecting these dots, I can feel an internal dialogue raging between the way I understood drugs and addiction before I met Joanne, and the things I've learned in the last couple of years.

For one, if the man hadn't broken the law, this family would never have been in this position! Doesn't the blame rest squarely on his shoulders? If you do the crime, be prepared to do the time. But as I've been on this journey of learning I've come to wonder if we're missing the other half of the story. Certainly, his choices will have natural consequences. He may have lost the relationships with his fiancée and daughter over time anyway, for any number of reasons. But prison is not a natural consequence. It's a proactive choice the community makes. He bears responsibility for his choices, but we bear responsibility for our response to his minor drug offense. I don't think he's the only one accountable for what just happened to his family.

The internal dialogue moves on to another conundrum. What about the people who say jail saved their life and was the catalyst for their sobriety? I've never heard that from someone who's actually still in jail, but I certainly believe that people who have this experience are telling the truth. It may very well be that jail did save their life. But like with the previous question of who bears responsibility, we tend to only look at one side of the coin. What about all the other stories of people for whom an arrest was the first domino in a chain reaction of suffering and loss? For every person who is arrested and comes out the other side with a story of positive change, there seem to be a hundred other people who experience the opposite. Am I willing to hear their stories too? Could the few people who were saved by jail also have been saved by another system that isn't so profoundly damaging to the many?

If prison ended drug use for the majority of people who spend time there, we simply wouldn't have the levels of drug use or addiction that we have. It just doesn't work that way. On my learning journey, I've heard a number of law enforcement officers share their perspectives, and one thing they all seem to agree on is how frustrating it is to arrest the same people over and over for drugs, and it doesn't solve the problem. Rat Park helped me understand why.

When we hear an amazing story of transformation through criminal justice involvement, we should celebrate and then ask,

"What about everyone else?" I like stories of redemption and restoration. They get traction on social media and are inspiring to tell friends over dinner. The stories of families sobbing in courtrooms and little girls growing up without a father are hard to hold. They're hidden, but they're happening every day. This could have been Joanne and Beckham.

The morning continues as I try to quiet my mind, with a conveyor belt of defendants coming in and out. Some of them get probation and are released while others head off to the warehouses of our prison system. There are thousands of courtrooms across America, cycling through lives just like this. Day after day. Year after year. After just two hours in one courtroom, I no longer wonder why Mississippi has the highest imprisonment rate in the country, or why the USA has one of the highest incarceration rates in the world.[2] One morning in one courtroom makes that abundantly clear.

Walking out to my Honda minivan after court, I glance a few parking places over and see the pregnant woman easing herself into her car. She arrived hoping to raise her daughter in a two-parent home. She left as a single mother. We can't always change people's behavior, but I wonder if we could change our response to drugs and addiction so it has a better chance of correcting problems without creating five more.

As I slip into the driver's seat, my heart is wrestling with what I saw this morning, and my mind is 100% convinced that jailing people just because they use drugs is doing much more harm than good. Being part of Joanne's journey has taught me that drug use is a health issue, not a criminal justice issue. Handling it as such would lead to much better outcomes than what I had just witnessed. Potentially harmful behavior like using drugs or even being addicted to them isn't the same thing as criminal behavior. It seems we've confused suffering people with dangerous people.

THE OTHER SIDE OF DRUG CRIMES

Even if I think people shouldn't be arrested for possessing drugs, what about people who truly are engaging in criminal behavior related to drugs, like violent gangs and cartels? I got curious about drugs because I wanted to understand Joanne. As I began learning about addiction, though, it was apparent pretty quickly that I had significantly underestimated just how much of our world is impacted by drugs and how we respond to them. Almost every area of our lives is touched. Learning about addiction catapulted me into the deep end of trying to understand harm related to drugs more broadly. The only way to solve a problem is to address the root of what's causing it, so I started learning everything I could about what causes crime and how to reduce it. The worried little girl who grew up at Loden Place listening to gunshots and police sirens as she lay in bed at night wanted answers to these questions. This little girl was in for a surprise…turns out addiction wasn't the only thing I had misunderstood.

CHAPTER 12

WE'VE BEEN HERE BEFORE

My hands are sweaty and my stomach is churning. A few weeks ago it sounded like a good idea to write an opinion article for our statewide newspaper. I wrote one last year about foster care that people really liked. Why not write one about all the new things I've been learning about drugs and addiction? It was published today, and a few seconds ago a friend texted saying, "Great article in the paper!" Now the vulnerability hangover is dragging me under. What have I done? Thousands of Mississippians might read something I wrote, on a very challenging topic, and I've never had thick skin. What if people tear me apart on social media? What if someone sends me an angry email? Why did I include my email address in the bio line!? Adrenaline is coursing through my body as I feel simultaneously proud and terrified.

I do get a few emails as the day moves on, but they're not angry. One of them is from a man I've never met named James Moore. He lives a couple of hours south of me and starts his email with, "Thank you for the courage of putting forth a very controversial notion of a proven more humane approach," and continues with his recommendation that I read the book *Chasing the Scream* - the very same book where I learned about Dr. Bruce Alexander's Rat Park experiments!

Over the next several years, I'll get to know James and hear his story. Many parts of it illustrate what I learned about the best way to reduce drug-related crime.

JAMES MOORE

When James Moore was 14 years old, his uncle, Raleigh, was the police chief in a small Alabama town. Even though alcohol prohibition had been repealed at the federal level almost 40 years earlier, the county Raleigh served in still prohibited selling or drinking it. Raleigh was never one to tell thrilling stories about his work even though he'd traveled the world in the Navy and served as a police officer in Miami for a year. He simply wanted to quietly serve this rural community, and enforcing alcohol prohibition was part of his job. Sometimes that meant crawling through briars to catch moonshiners, and other times it meant busting a juke joint where alcohol was flowing.

One day he got a tip about alcohol at a local juke joint and drove out to do his job. As he walked in someone yelled, "Police!" and pandemonium broke out. Two people grabbed his arms and tried to get his gun. During the struggle, a third shot him in the head. Even though another officer arrived on the scene and rushed him to the hospital, Raleigh slipped into a coma and died a week later, leaving a young wife and unborn child.

James remembers his mom opening his bedroom door that day. He thought she was coming to tell him to turn down the music he was blasting. Instead, she told him his beloved uncle had been shot. James was close to his uncle and was devastated when he died. At the funeral, James stayed outside so no one would see him crying. As far as he could see, a ribbon of squad cars lined the road as officers from all over the state packed the country church to honor Raleigh's life and sacrifice.

The tragedy deepened James' respect for law enforcement and the job they were doing to rid communities of the menace of drugs and alcohol. He didn't wait long to join them.

As a 17-year-old college freshman at the University of Southern Mississippi, James volunteered to be an undercover informant for the local Narcotics Task Force. It was 1974 and James saw it as an opportunity to help rid his community of drugs. His long hair, beard, and recently purchased motorcycle would even help him fit in at the pool halls he would be frequenting in his new role.

His job was to build up enough trust with someone to buy drugs from them so the task force could arrest the dealer. Although James volunteered, many informants today are people who get arrested on a drug charge and agree to set up a few other people for arrest in exchange for their own charges getting dropped. Whether voluntary or coerced, informant work is dangerous. People don't take kindly to being double-crossed, so James had to check in every day with the agent managing him so they could make sure he was alive and well.

Sunday afternoons were now spent at the local pool halls, though James kept an eye on the time so he could get to church by 5:30 to direct the children's choir. When the day came for his first drug purchase, everything went off without a hitch. James gave the dealer $30 and got a baggie of marijuana laced with heroin. He was elated! Some drugs and a dealer would be off the street.

Unfortunately, an hour later when they tested the drugs back at the task force office, there was no trace of marijuana or heroin. Instead, the taxpayers just purchased $30 of oregano with baby powder sprinkled on it. Big problem. It wasn't just disappointing that no arrest could be made. James now had a credibility problem. If he shrugged off the fake drugs, the dealer would be suspicious and it would jeopardize his cover. So the Narcotics Task Force sent an undercover agent back to the scene along with James to confront the dealer. He was too nervous to go alone. As soon as the dealer opened his mouth to protest the accusation of fake drugs, the undercover agent broke a pool stick over the dealer's back and threw him through the wood-paneled wall. James looked on in stunned silence as other patrons of the pool hall pulled out their wallets and covered the $30. The agent and James grabbed the money and sped off, but his cover was blown and he started getting death threats. After some very tense days with James going to live with a professor for his safety, the task force found the source of the threats and his life slowly returned to normal. His informant work was over, but his interest in police work to rid the community of drugs continued.

DRUG DEALING, CRIME, AND LAW ENFORCEMENT

The problem of crime and drug dealing was one of the hardest for me to sort out. My experience with Joanne helped me see people through a more compassionate lens, especially those who suffered from addiction. Yet my compassion fell short when it came to those dealing drugs...people who had made my street feel unsafe when I was growing up...people who seemed bent on making a profit no matter what it meant or what it took. The last thing I wanted was a soft approach to that! I just wanted less crime. James Moore's story helps illustrate an unexpected path to that very thing.

James' uncle experienced the reality that alcohol prohibition didn't stop the production or consumption of alcohol. Any time there is demand for a product, there will always be someone willing to supply it. If legal businesses aren't allowed to, illegal ones will. Certainly, alcohol prohibition deterred some people from drinking, but there was still a huge demand for alcohol. In the absence of legal options, an illegal market launched and thrived. Crime was rewarded because only people willing to break the law could get a share of the profits. Thinking about the murder of James' uncle, I think it's short-sighted to think of justice only through the lens of punishing the people who committed the act. Certainly, they should be punished, no question. But what was the root cause? What led to that altercation? What incentivized that kind of violence? In his case, it was alcohol prohibition that sparked the tip-off to the police. Prohibition also gave them the job of breaking up that illegal activity, sending James' uncle into a dangerous situation. And prohibition ignited the fear of arrest that led to a violent reaction in the juke joint. Without prohibition, that altercation never would have happened. Sometimes I think we're so focused on enforcing laws and punishing crime that we lose sight of what prevents it in the first place. Shouldn't the goal be *less crime?*

Even though alcohol prohibition has largely ended, the prohibition of other drugs has created a replica personal safety problem for law enforcement officers. James got a taste of this during his informant work. Many officers lose their lives today enforcing the prohibition of other drugs, just as officers like Raleigh did in decades past enforcing alcohol prohibition.

I've always been thankful for law enforcement. If there was one comfort to me as a little girl struggling with anxiety about crime, it was knowing that I could call 911 and get help. One afternoon not long after the robbery, I was hanging laundry out on the clothesline. We had a washing machine but no dryer, so this was a regular job for me. From our yard, I could see through the neighbor's yard to Clinton Boulevard, an east-west thoroughfare through Jackson. Funerals regularly came past, but today as I hung up our clothes it was a law enforcement officer's funeral that slowly processed past. I stopped my work and stood quietly. Dad had taught us the proper way to salute from his years in the military, and I felt a strong desire to stand at attention and salute as I watched that funeral pass, though I was worried one of my brothers or a neighbor kid would see me and laugh. Instead, I stood solemnly and waited to finish hanging the laundry until the last squad car passed.

Now an adult, I know that not all police officers are trustworthy and not all police cultures are healthy. But that hasn't changed my conviction that law enforcement plays a crucial role in society. I believed it all those years ago at Loden Place, and

I believe it now. What's changed is my understanding of what happens when popular drugs are prohibited. It creates violence against law enforcement and a public safety disaster for all of us.

CHAPTER 13

THE WRONG WINNERS

When I was just a toddler, Mom and Dad took their one and only entrepreneurial leap. Dad worked full-time at Mt. Salus Christian School, Mom was a homemaker, and they started their version of a side hustle. The business was called The Garage Sale Guide. Every weekend, Dad got a list of all the garage sales advertised in the newspaper (or yard sales, tag sales, whatever your part of the country calls them), then painstakingly marked the location of each one on a map of the city. He printed paid business advertisements on the edges of the map and delivered the finished maps to area gas stations. Garage sale lovers could pick one up for free and have all the area garage sales mapped out for them. As someone who loves garage sales, I still think this is an ingenious idea. Unfortunately, although they worked their tails off, the product never caught on. Mom and Dad couldn't sell enough advertisements to make The Garage Sale Guide profitable, and the business went under. They were living the reality that no matter how badly they wanted to supply their product, there simply wasn't enough demand for it. Demand drives supply.

But let's say The Garage Sale Guide had been wildly successful; consumers loved it and advertisers were clamoring to get a spot on the edge of that map. Demand was high. Quite likely the Garage Sale Gurus would have sprung up with their own map to compete with the Garage Sale Guide. Demand for a product translates into dollar signs for anyone willing to supply it. Humans aren't very good at leaving piles of cash untouched, so there tends to be an endless supply of people willing to produce anything that consumers want. That's true of legal products and services, but it's also true of illegal ones. I grew up thinking we could decrease the demand for drugs by decreasing the supply. Turns out, it works the other way around.

Picture tens of millions of consumers holding out hundreds of billions of dollars every year to anyone who will sell them the drugs they want. There's just one problem. Currently, the drugs they want are illegal, so this huge pile of consumer cash can only be earned by people breaking the law. That's the scenario that drug prohibition sets up. It incentivizes crime by forcing an extremely lucrative market underground, luring people into criminal activity who might have been used car salesmen or electricians if being a drug dealer didn't pay so much more.

All my life I heard that drugs cause crime. It took some focused learning to understand why the underground market - not the drugs - is actually responsible for the vast majority of the crime.

That huge pile of consumer cash is why if you arrest 100 drug dealers, 100 more take their place by the end of the day. If you arrest them the next day, 100 more will take their place. No amount of incarceration will stop people from taking the risk to cash in. Corrupt character isn't the driving force behind people selling illegal drugs. Cash is. The previous dealers may be behind bars, but a whole new group of people just got lured into illegal activity.

Similarly, seizing drugs doesn't stop the sale of drugs. Daniel Snyder, a friend I met on this learning journey, saw the challenge of trying to stop the drug supply firsthand during his 2 decades of heroin addiction. He later told me, "Drugs are not hard to obtain. Never in my years and years of drug use was it hard to get drugs." Even when law enforcement seized huge quantities of drugs, Daniel said, "They've never interrupted the drug supply. The void is filled immediately. We knew that as users. There was always someone else waiting. No one had a worry that one day all the police would get all the drugs."

The public may feel good when they see a news story about a drug dealer being arrested or bags of fentanyl taken off the street. But arresting a drug dealer doesn't stop the sale of drugs. Neither does seizing a shipment of them. In the same way that a business like Walmart knows how much merchandise they'll lose to shoplifting, drug trafficking organizations know how much of their product will be seized. Both are sophisticated multi-billion dollar business operations. Both simply ship more products on the front end to make up for what they know they'll lose.

If we locked up every drug dealer on earth today, they would all be replaced immediately. If we seized every shipment of drugs on earth, it would be replaced in no time. Consumers still want drugs and are still holding out hundreds of billions of dollars to anyone willing to supply them.

I think the term "drug war" that was popularized in the 1970s has really done a disservice to us. Wars can be won. With enough manpower and resources, it's possible to end the conflict by subduing the enemy. But the so-called "drug war" does not work this way because we are fighting dealers, gangs, cartels, and drugs...when the real challenge is economics! There is an unchanging reality of drug supply and drug demand, and no war will ever make it stop or go away; this type of fight can't be won.

DOMINO EFFECT

Just like alcohol prohibition didn't stop alcohol from being manufactured, sold, and consumed, the prohibition of other drugs hasn't stopped them either. Again, making drugs like marijuana, cocaine, or heroin illegal has certainly deterred some people from using them. But the US government estimates that 15% of American adults have used an illegal drug recently.[3] That's an awful lot of people who are shrugging their shoulders at the government's decision to make a drug illegal. With all those consumers holding out their money to anyone who will supply them with their drug of choice, it is 100% predictable that a thriving underground market will form. Just like it did during alcohol prohibition. If the goal is to have fewer people engaged in criminal activity, prohibition is the definition of a failed policy. But the cycle continues. Decade after decade.

As I began to get my mind around these ideas, I saw that prohibiting popular drugs isn't fighting crime. It's creating it. And not just in theory.

Thinking back to James Moore's experience as a 17-year-old in that pool hall, what would his options have been if he was a regular customer instead of an informant when his dealer sold him that baggie of fake drugs? Calling the police isn't an option. Suing the dealer for ripping him off isn't an option either. Consumers can do both of these with legal businesses. But for James, his only options would have been to let the dealer rip him off or confront the dealer himself.

When a market can't operate legally, the only way to settle disputes is through force instead of litigation. That's true for the relationship between consumers and dealers, and it's also true of disputes between dealers. The more violent someone selling drugs is - killing competitors, for instance - the more territory and supply routes they can control. That means more of that pile of consumer cash will be theirs. Making popular drugs illegal is like giving organized crime a winning lottery ticket. A never-ending windfall of cash now flows into the coffers of gangs, cartels, and terrorist organizations, who fight over it on the streets of our cities every day. The more ruthless and violent you are, the richer you'll be.

If public safety is the goal, drug prohibition is a spectacular backfire.

Politicians talk about ending drug dealing by giving out longer prison sentences or even instituting the death penalty for it. But people engaged in a lawless underground market have already factored in the risk of death, and it's a risk they're obviously willing to take. If the immediate risk of death embedded in the underground market isn't stopping them, why would a few more years in prison or even death through the legal system? That mountain of cash speaks pretty loudly.

In all of this mess, one bright spot shines in my mind. Underground markets can get a lot by force, but there's one key thing they can't: customers. The history of alcohol in this country shows us that most people don't want to buy their drugs from someone on a street corner. The Al Capones of the 1920s didn't give up their revenue stream by choice. They were put out of business by *customer*s who chose to buy *legal* alcohol when it was available again. Customers with no other options will continue buying from criminal organizations. Customers with *viable* legal options won't. The underground market can't make money as consumer buying habits and cash switch back to the legal market. Consider illicit alcohol…its demand all but vanished when legal access was implemented again. Bankrupting criminal organizations is a much more effective way of fighting them than actually fighting them.

Just like my parents couldn't sell The Garage Sale Guide to customers who didn't want it, criminal organizations can't sell drugs to customers that won't buy them. With no customers, there's no cash to pay for weapons, ammunition, housing, food, vehicles, etc. Gangs, cartels, and terrorist organizations would have a fraction of the influence, power, and breadth of impact they do today if drug prohibition wasn't giving them an operational budget of several hundred billion dollars a year. You can't force people not to engage in criminal activity, but you can at least make it a volunteer enterprise. Opening up legal markets for drugs to be sold to adults would be an effective way to defund the cartels. It's like beating them at their own game.

It's shocking to me how much crime and violence on a global scale is so utterly preventable. The alcohol market today gives us a glimpse of what's possible. CEOs of alcohol corporations aren't plotting the kidnapping and execution of each other's employees. Liquor store owners aren't plotting to kill each other before sporting events in the name of beer sales. We can't even imagine such a thing because it's so ludicrous. But that's exactly what happened in the United States during the days of alcohol prohibition. Thankfully, it doesn't happen today because laws changed. Alcohol is still alcohol, but now it is legal and regulated instead of illegal and prohibited. The violent underground market for it is no longer a problem. I wish we could say the same of the market for other drugs.

As I started to pay attention to news stories about crime, it was mind blowing to realize just how often the root cause was tied to drug prohibition. Violent altercations with law enforcement often started with a search for drugs during a traffic stop or a raid on a home. Murders were often linked back to drug dealing. And the underground market south of the United States border has funneled so much money to cartels that whole countries are rocked by violence and corruption, causing millions of people to flee north. Truly, the public safety disaster spawned by drug prohibition spans the globe.

The more I learned about prohibition, crime, and addiction, the more I realized how skewed my understanding of these had been for most of my life. However, the rest of James Moore's story shows how the consequences of drug prohibition right now don't just seep into our communities. They make their way into our homes.

CHAPTER 14

THE FLIPSIDE OF FENTANYL

My flip-flops thump against my heels as I walk out of the restroom at the baseball field, my 4-year-old son Brandon next to me. It's been six months since we finalized his adoption, and although there's so much loss that's also wrapped up in adoption, we're overjoyed that we get to experience the gift of him being part of our family forever.

Thomas, Cole, Brandon and I are watching 8-year-old Tyson play ball on this warm spring afternoon. The restrooms are on the back of the cinderblock building that houses the concession stand. Not even a Mississippi tornado could take this building down. The restroom doors alone feel like they weigh 50 pounds. As we walk out the door, I turn left to go around to the front of the building and toward Tyson's field. Brandon does the same, but he slips his fingers into the crack close to the hinges and pivots himself around the door jam. Before I can react the door slams, taking the top of Brandon's finger off. He screams as I rush him back inside to grab paper towels and try to control the blood. Determined to channel the same commitment to calm that I had during the train wreck, I don't scream or cry. I talk to him calmly and lead him outside, where I call to other parents watching their kids play. Surely someone here is a doctor or nurse who can tell me what to do.

Just because I'm not panicking doesn't mean I'm thinking clearly. I can't figure out what the next step is. How do I find Thomas, who's at a field out of sight? What do I do with Brandon? Thankfully there's a doctor at a nearby field, and he looks at Brandon's finger while another parent runs to find Thomas. The finger looks so strange, but my mind is blank and it doesn't register that what I'm looking at is an exposed bone. Thomas comes running around the corner, also in shock. The doctor helps us push through our frozen state by telling us we need to leave *now* and get him to the Emergency Room. Thankfully the children's hospital is only a mile away. We're taken to an exam room and a smiling nurse appears with a syringe. She cheerfully tells us she's going to give him some fentanyl to help with the pain. Wait a second. Did she just say fentanyl? This is 2019 and people are dying of overdose from the synthetic opioid fentanyl in record numbers across the country. It's all over the news. How is it, then, that my 4-year-old can take fentanyl and feel better while he gets stitches, when grown men are dying from it? It's a question James Moore was asking for a different reason.

JAMES AND JEFFREY

One winter afternoon in 1997, as the temperature hovered around 40 degrees, James Moore took his 7-year-old son Jeffrey fishing on the lake at Turkey Fork. A few years earlier James bought their first boat, but it was so unreliable that they often said they were just going for a drive to the lake. If the boat happened to start, that was icing on the cake. Now they'd upgraded to a pontoon boat with a safety railing around all of it except for about 2 feet by the ladder. Somehow, that day little Jeffrey still managed to fall in the frigid water as he fished. James, a stickler for safety, hauled him back into the boat by his life jacket, with Jeffrey still clutching his rod and reel. Not expecting anyone to get wet, James hadn't brought a towel, much less a blanket or extra clothes. He stripped Jeffrey down to his underwear, rung out his clothes, and did the only thing he could think to do - dry them as quickly as possible. A half-naked Jeffrey clung to the railing, shaking with cold, as James turned the boat full throttle, drying the clothes as they looped the lake.

James chuckles as he tells me that story. It's one of his favorites from Jeffrey's childhood.

We've had many conversations since his initial email thanking me for my opinion article in the paper. Through our friendship, I heard about his experiences as an informant as well as his uncle's sacrifice as a police officer enforcing alcohol prohibition. But it is his experience as Jeffrey's father that has most shaped James and his view of drugs.

After finishing college and getting married to his wife Jan, James took his love of cycling and the $2200 in his retirement account and opened Moore's Bike Shop as his day job. Fulfilling his dream of honoring his uncle's life through service in law enforcement, he worked at night as a reserve police officer and eventually a part-time officer. Any time they caught someone with drugs, James felt proud. They were making the community safer by getting drugs, dealers, and users off the street. The same year James became a reserve officer, his son Jeffrey was born. As Jeffrey got older, James' journey to stop harm from drugs accelerated and took some unexpected twists. Twists that help us understand why so many people are dying from drug overdose and how we can save their lives.

Jeffrey was a happy, kind child who was loved by his teachers and friends. By 8th grade, he was in the gifted program at school. In 9th grade he branched out into band and show choir, excelling there too. But he also struggled with anxiety that became more prominent as he hit middle school. Before long James found empty beer cans, a half bottle of fingernail polish remover, and paint-soaked rags stuffed in plastic bags in Jeffrey's room.

James began noticing Jeffrey's dilated pupils when he came home after hanging out with his friends. Sometimes his face was red and splotchy. James brushed it off. Jeffrey always had an explanation, and James knew his son had overheard stories of his dad busting people for drugs as a cop. Jeffrey knew how deeply anti-drug his dad was. But as high school progressed, Jeffrey's grades started slipping as he slipped into addiction. He dropped out of the band and show choir, barely graduating. Then money disappeared and eventually Jeffrey confessed to stealing it. Tension grew as Jeffrey's addiction took its toll on his relationships as well as his dependability as an employee at the family bike shop.

James was crushed as he watched his son's life spiral, and he often did what many parents do. He lashed out in anger, trying to correct what he saw as a behavior problem. "I dealt with him with a firm hand," James says, "to the point that his fear was 'my dad will kill me if he finds this out.'" Judgment and arguments became a fixture in their relationship even after Jeffrey moved out on his own, but they didn't stop Jeffrey's drug use.

One night in particular sticks out in James' mind as an example of the roller coaster they were on. James walked into Jeffrey's house when he thought Jeffrey had stopped using and was sober. He saw a hypodermic needle on the kitchen table, loaded with drugs. "I yelled, I screamed, I cursed, and I threw things," James remembers. It made no difference. Jeffrey's battle with addiction raged on, as did James' battle with Jeffrey. As year after year of this cycle came and went, continued trips to the lake to fish became one of their only lifelines of connection.

One of those trips happened a few months after Jeffrey graduated from the local junior college on the president's list, in spite of his injection heroin use. James and Jeffrey went to their favorite lake on a weekday morning, stopping at a small-town gas station to get some fried chicken to eat while they fished. James still won't tell me the name of the lake because nobody ever goes there and he wants it to stay that way.

As they were launching their boat, they noticed a sign by the lake. It warned of an alligator sighting and gave two instructions. Do not approach. Do not disturb. So, James tells me with a laugh, they launched their boat with two goals in mind. Approach and disturb the alligator. They spotted him on the bank as they came around a point, and watched all 8 feet of him slide into the water. Staying true to their goals, James cast his fishing line out toward the gator, finally getting the hook to catch behind the gator's head. Almost immediately they felt their boat being tugged along as the gator swam away from them on the surface of the water. James heard Jeffrey giggling from the back of the boat and turned to find him videoing the scene with his phone. All was well until the gator made a 180-degree turn and came straight for the boat. The video ends with father and son yelling and scrambling to start the motor and hightail it out of there while the phone clatters into the bottom of the boat. Through the storm of addiction, they were still able to share moments of sunlight, making some good memories together.

A few weeks later, Jeffrey told James he was ready for in-patient treatment for his drug addiction. After 10 years of the roller coaster, Jeffrey was finally ready for recovery. He got a spot in a local drug treatment center, and James and his wife went to visit Jeffrey every Saturday. They noticed he was gaining weight and seemed to be much more stable. But on day 60 of his stay in treatment, James got a call. Jeffrey was caught smoking a cigarette for the 4th time, and the program kicked him out. James was livid. How could a facility that treats addiction expel his son for struggling with an addiction? It made no sense.

James arrived at the treatment center to find Jeffrey sitting in the lobby with his bags packed beside him. They drove home for yet another family meeting. Jeffrey agreed to continue his treatment at another center in the area, so James immediately called to see if Jeffrey could start the same day. Miraculously, they had a spot! All James needed was approval from his insurance company, but he couldn't get anyone to answer so he left a message on the answering machine. For the rest of the afternoon, they called repeatedly, even driving to the new treatment center to sit in the parking lot in case the insurance company called back with approval before the center's intake office closed at 5:00 pm. No call.

Disappointed, they drove back home, but James felt desperate. The next morning he told Jeffrey to get in the truck. They were going to the new treatment center and they'd worry about how to pay for it later. Jeffrey's still-packed bags went back in the truck and they were off. But something had changed. As they drove, Jeffrey told James he could stay sober on his own. Sixty days were long enough, he said. James was adamant. Jeffrey needed to finish treatment. At the next red light, Jeffrey hopped out of the truck and started walking down the road. The window of opportunity had closed. He was done with treatment.

Several days later, on a spring morning in April, Jeffrey was supposed to meet his mom at their church to use the computer and fill out some job applications. When he missed that appointment, James got worried. He picked his wife, Jan, up and they went to Jeffrey's house. "I called his name, and I went into the living room and saw him laying on the sofa. It just looked like he was asleep," James remembers. "When I called his name again and he didn't move, it hit me." He yelled for Jan to call 911 as he pulled Jeffrey onto the floor and started CPR. "I knew at that point that it was too late," James says, wiping away tears as he tells me this part of their journey. And it was. Jeffrey died from an overdose of heroin laced with fentanyl. He was just 24.

How do you even capture the grief of a parent losing a child? There are no words wide and deep enough to express it.

JEFFREY LEE MOORE
MAY 17, 1990 - APRIL 6, 2015

The day after Jeffrey died, James was sitting with Jan at the funeral home, writing Jeffrey's obituary with the funeral director, when his cell phone rang. It was their insurance company, calling back to get Jeffrey into the second treatment center. The woman who verifies eligibility had been on vacation when James called before.

It stings just hearing this story; I cannot imagine what James and Jan felt after they hung up the phone. How can one too many cigarettes and a vacation day turn the tide and be the difference between life and death? As James continues telling me the story, I realize for the first time the extreme, persistent stress that families face when their loved one struggles with addiction.

On their way to church for Jeffrey's funeral, James and Jan passed the treatment center he had been kicked out of. The parking lot was filled with cars. It was the beginning of Family Week when the loved ones of people in treatment got to participate in several days of activities. Instead of pulling into the parking lot to spend time with Jeffrey, they continued down the road to attend his funeral.

The church was full of family and friends, including many of Jeffrey's friends who also struggled with addictions. As James and Jan walked past the urn holding Jeffrey's ashes, James reached out and placed his hand on it for a moment. How do you say goodbye to your beloved son who should still be here?

PREVENTABLE HARM

Jeffrey passed away 8 months before I met Joanne. By the time I met James Moore and heard his story several years later, we had been on similar learning journeys. We'd both concluded that it was futile to focus on drugs if we want to reduce addiction. "I'm not sure that the drugs were the problem so much as the symptom of a problem," James says, as he reflects on the root causes of Jeffrey's struggle. He now describes problematic drug use as "A way to turn down the volume of the things that are hurting you." Sounds a lot like what Dr. Bruce Alexander learned 50 years ago. Both of us were also convinced that criminalizing drugs was causing a massive amount of preventable crime.

The last piece of the puzzle was the overdose crisis, something James paid the ultimate price for. The history of alcohol prohibition as well as our very different experiences with fentanyl illustrate the root cause of the overdose crisis in two ways.

First, prohibiting a drug removes the option for any kind of quality control and introduces rampant contamination. Before alcohol prohibition, there was quality controlled alcohol on the shelves of legal businesses, just like there is today. But during prohibition, there was no labeling and no regulation. People were selling whatever they cooked up in their bathtubs or out in the woods behind their houses. I always thought of prohibition as the ultimate form of regulation, but now I see it's really the absence of any form of regulation. It's a complete free-for-all.

Second, prohibiting a drug incentivizes the sale of higher-potency formulations. This principle, often called the Iron Law of Prohibition, plays out today at sports stadiums where alcohol is prohibited. Outside, people tailgate with beer. But inside, where alcohol is prohibited, they start drinking hard liquor. They're facing the same dilemma all underground drug markets face. If you have to smuggle an intoxicant, you want the biggest punch in the smallest package. No one at the football game is going to take the risk of smuggling in a case of beer when they could smuggle a flask of liquor and get the same effect. When a drug becomes illegal, size matters.

When effective smuggling is key to your business model, as it is with drug trafficking today, small packages translate to big dollar signs. If college football fans respond to the potency incentives of prohibition, it should come as no surprise that criminal enterprises do too.

Prohibition incentivizes high-potency drugs and enables rampant contamination, which leads to people buying a baggie of who-knows-what on the street. It's a coin flip. Will they get high or die? There's no way to know.

Today, fentanyl increases potency while decreasing smuggling risk. It packs that all-important punch in a minuscule package. But it won't end with fentanyl. Next year it might be carfentanyl, which is 100 times more potent than fentanyl. Or xylazine, a large animal tranquilizer already showing up across the country. Or nitazenes.

The key to understanding the fentanyl overdose crisis is realizing it's not about fentanyl or any of the other drugs continuously emerging in the underground market. It isn't the drug that kills people, per se. It's the dose. Brandon's nurse in the ER had access to pure fentanyl, which has been used in helpful ways in medical settings every day for decades. His nurse knew exactly how much to give a 4-year-old to help with his pain. But that's a completely different situation from drugs on the street.

Without quality control and accurate labeling, people like Jeffrey Moore have no way of appropriately dosing what they're using and are dying because of it. Countless people will buy drugs illegally today, and two hundred and seventy-five of them will die from an overdose. Most of those are preventable if the person simply knows the potency and ingredients of the drug they're using. Prohibition makes this impossible. Jeffrey's dad, James, sees this and says, "It's the policies that are as much responsible for the death as it is the substance that stopped the heart. Perhaps more so."

As we put the pieces of the puzzle together, we both saw a very different picture than the one we expected. It reminds me of a favorite memory from one of the trips Mom and I took when she was sick.

CHAPTER 15

PANORAMA

My hiking boots feel heavy on my feet as I follow the path through the trees and up the mountain. Mom's boots make little dust puffs in front of me, and her voice rings out across the side of the mountain as she sings "The Happy Wanderer," putting special emphasis on the last line, "My knapsack on my back!" We've run through a bunch of songs by this time, both of us singing at the top of our lungs to scare off bears in the area.

We're staying in Colorado for a few days at the Eden Valley Institute which is below us in the valley. Mom is in the middle of a good window of health on her cancer journey so she and I are on an epic seven-week adventure visiting family and sites throughout Iowa, Colorado, and Washington State. It's my senior year of high school, but because I'm homeschooled we can be creative with my schedule, making this trip in the fall of 2000 possible. Mom and Dad came to Eden Valley alone already when the Christian healthcare sharing program they're part of decided to send them in case alternative treatments would be effective at fighting Mom's cancer. She wanted me to experience the beauty of the valley and the mountain, so we stopped in for a couple of nights just to go hiking together.

Last night at dinner one of the institute employees told us the story of hiking on the mountain and being chased by a bear. He climbed a tree but the bear climbed after him. He still has the boots with the bear's teeth marks from those harrowing moments as he clung to the tree, kicking at the bear below him. That was enough to scare the daylights out of me, so I'm dutifully singing at the top of my lungs along with Mom as we hike. Two inexperienced hikers happening upon a bear seems like a recipe for bear lunch. But this is Mom in her element. She loves an adventure, as long as there are birds to watch and nature to enjoy. Her binoculars are hanging around her neck, as they so often do when she's outside. She's always ready to glue them to her eyeballs when a flash of movement on a tree branch or some rustling leaves signals there's a bird to be found and identified.

We finally come to the top of the mountain. As we come out of the trees and onto open rock, the wind grabs my hat. When Mom and Dad came up here several months ago they got burned to a crisp as they sat and enjoyed the view, so we're prepared for the sun today. The wind is so strong, though, that my hat won't stay on. Mom, whose skills at improvising have been well-honed by a lifetime of frugal living, figures out a way to wind my fanny pack around my head and secure my hat with it. I wouldn't have been caught dead with a fanny pack at home, but this one is left over from a mission trip I took last summer to Honduras where it was the safest way to carry money, and Mom thought it would come in handy because we would be doing so much walking and hiking on this trip. I look ridiculous but it's just us and the bears up here.

We carefully climb up several rocks and scoot along carefully as a breathtaking view opens up. We can see for miles all around out to the horizon, including a stomach-churning view straight down to a hidden green valley far below. I see why we climbed so carefully at the top. We're not on the top of a mountain so much as we are on the edge of a ledge. All the individual sections we hiked through are part of one panoramic view up here. It's a completely different perspective and it's stunning.

Mom isn't the kind of person who just wants to see something beautiful. She wants to pull out a lawn chair and soak it in. We didn't take any lawn chairs with us up the mountain, but we settle in for a few hours of soaking. We eat a snack and then sing all Mom's favorite hymns. We already cycled through some of them on the hike up, as we racked our brains for every song we could remember words to, but one of Mom's traditions since she got cancer is to sing all her favorite hymns when she's in a place that strikes awe and wonder in her. We sing through "Praise to the Lord the Almighty," "Beautiful Savior," "Crown Him with Many Crowns" and the others before she pulls out her journal and I open my latest novel as we bask in God's glorious creation.

THE BIG PICTURE

Those hours on the top of the mountain with Mom gave me a panoramic view of a landscape that most people only see small pieces of. On the learning journey after I met Joanne, I felt like I was climbing that mountain. I saw different pieces of the puzzle of drugs and addiction, but it was like catching a glimpse of sky, then walking through a little meadow, then snaking through trees. I had to get way up on the mountain through a lot of learning before I could see all those pieces together as one landscape spread out in front of me. Getting to this panoramic view has been crucial. If I only see crime or only see people dying from fentanyl or only see the chaotic behavior of someone struggling with addiction, my conclusion about the solution is very limited. Zooming out and seeing all the pieces together unlocks a new point of view for me that I can't unsee.

I got interested in the issue of drugs and addiction because I care about people, not because I care about drugs. I've still never used an illegal drug, never tried marijuana, and don't even drink alcohol. My gaze has stayed on the issue of drugs because at every turn I see that how we handle drugs is deeply tied to the healing or harm of individuals, families, and communities. It's tied to people like the pregnant woman in that courtroom and her unborn daughter. To people like Payton and James Moore and Joanne. To people like you and me. Brian Gault, a pastor friend, says he believes the human longing for justice is really a longing for beauty…for things to be right and good and beautiful, as they were meant to be. This desire for a restoration of goodness and beauty resonates with my own motivation to keep learning about drugs and addiction.

As I put the pieces of the puzzle together in my mind, I see how in the past I've only had one label for all harm even remotely associated with drugs. Crime, addiction, broken families, overdose - I labeled it all "Harm From Drugs." Now I see that a lot of those harms are created or exacerbated by using the criminal justice system to address drugs. We've been blaming drugs for harm largely caused by our drug policies.

Banning drugs isn't reducing crime, it's rewarding it.

Incarcerating people who use drugs isn't reducing addiction, it's fueling it.

Forcing various drugs out of regulation isn't preventing overdose, it's causing it.

As each of these become clear to me, I struggle to see how continuing to use the criminal justice system to address drugs is the path forward if life, health, sobriety, and public safety are important. My support for a criminal justice approach to drugs, prior to meeting Joanne, hinged on the belief that it was reducing harm. Instead, it seems to be turning a campfire into a forest fire. Surely there is a better way to uphold the sanctity of life and the image of God.

A friend that I was discussing these ideas with commented to me that we don't want to change anything too quickly or we're going to "lose people off the ship." He has a fair concern; however, right now preventable crime, overdose from contamination, and incarceration are resulting in tens of thousands of people being "thrown overboard" every year. We're not in neutral. We need to consider the risks of change, but we have to consider the cost of the status quo just as deeply.

As I reflect on everything I've learned about drugs and addiction, I realize that I've learned two very important things: First, my values *aren't* changing. I'm still a conservative Christian mother who is more comprehensively pro-life after this journey than I've ever been. Second, my perspective on the solutions that best align with those values *is* changing. For most of my life, I thought the only people who wanted to stop using the criminal justice system to handle drugs were people who wanted to use drugs. I guess I've always thought there are two options with drugs: ban them or celebrate them. Now I see a third way supported by a growing group of people, like James and me, who don't want people using drugs *and* see that the current policies have increased harm in the market, to the substance, and to consumers. We're losing on every front. If we don't change our strategy, the loss of life, damage to families, and detriment to society will multiply and affect each and every one of us even more than it is today.

SHIFTING

I realize a shift is taking place in me. Like most people, I've always loved stories of "restoration after harm"...Joanne getting Beckham back falls into such a category, I suppose. But now I'm also gaining a vision for the *prevention* of harm. They are both good, but they are very different approaches.

Maybe we love restoration stories because we're in the middle of God's epic restoration story and we recognize how badly our world needs it. How deeply marred it is. The downside of a good restoration story, though, is that brokenness has to happen first. A person working an 8-5 job with a spouse and two kids is boring unless they were living on the street before. Then we cheer. Someone paying for their groceries on a Saturday afternoon doesn't even register in our minds as impressive unless previously they spent their last dollar on heroin. Then we celebrate. Someone coaching their kid's baseball team and mentoring local youth doesn't get anyone talking unless they were a drug dealer who went to prison and had an awakening. Then we get inspired.

Only after disaster strikes is there a gripping story of transformation to tell. When we go upriver and prevent harm in the first place, there's no story. Changing our approach to drugs would be an effort to make stories of brokenness a lot less common. It would make drug production, sales, and use a lot more boring. Can we celebrate and work toward the prevention of harm as much as we do the restoration after harm? Prevention may not make the news like restoration does, but it can be even more transformative. We can't just look for *where* brokenness exists and then try to restore it. We have to ask *why* it happened and try to stop it before it hurts someone else.

A big piece that feels foundational to my understanding of the world, people, and public policy has crumbled since I met Joanne. This learning journey hasn't felt like a great adventure. It's been really stressful to consider new information. To figure out how it impacts my current worldview and values. To sort through the changes it might lead to. Sometimes I feel energized by something like Rat Park that gives me insight I haven't had before. But on the whole, it feels like the rug has gotten ripped out from under me and I'm not quite certain which way is up. What do I do with this paradigm shift?

A memory from Loden Place surfaces. I'm a little girl, it's Sunday night, and my 3 brothers and I are gathered with Mom and Dad for our nightly Bible reading and prayer. Dad reads us something that will shine a light on my path forward today.

PART III:
LASTING SOLUTIONS

CHAPTER 16

CHANGING COURSE

"Devotions!" I hear Dad call from the living room. I pack up the pearler beads I've been making designs with at the kitchen table as my brothers tromp into the living room for our nightly family Bible reading and prayer. We read a chapter of the Bible every night, us kids splitting up all the verses to read aloud. When there's an uneven number I get to read the least amount since I'm the youngest. Because of this, I've known how to pronounce "Philistines" and "Methuselah" since I could add and subtract. But tonight is different because it's Sunday. On Sunday nights we practice memorizing Bible passages like Psalm 103 and Psalm 15, and Dad reads us letters from missionaries around the world that our family supports. It's my favorite night of devotions. One of the missionaries works in a country where security is a big issue and Christians are persecuted, so they always give updates on the people they work with by calling them by their occupation, such as the Orange Juice Salesman. That makes their work feel even more intriguing.

Mom, Dad, the boys and I pack into our postage stamp living room with the usual amount of fighting among us kids over who's sitting in whose favorite seat and whose foot is touching someone else. As we quiet down, Dad pulls out a ministry update to read to us. This one's different, though. It's from an organization that provides help in crisis situations. They send out letters telling their readers about a particular one-time need, and the readers each send in $5 to help meet it. It might be help for people who have been displaced by a tsunami or for missionaries who need a new vehicle. But tonight's letter isn't about a new need, it's about a past one. Several months before, we got a letter explaining that there was a huge problem with human slavery in a particular country, and for a certain amount of money the organization could buy the freedom of enslaved people. They asked everyone to send in their $5 so they could free as many people as possible, and readers responded. Tonight as Dad reads, it becomes immediately clear that there's a problem. The slave traders responded too. As soon as they realized there was a profit to be made in selling slaves back into freedom, they ramped up their kidnapping operation for the express purpose of selling the slaves back to the ministry. A solution that was implemented with the best of intentions actually created worse problems. Now even more people were being forced into slavery. Instead of fighting slavery, the influx of cash incentivized even more of it.

The letter ended with the update that the slave-buying ministry was over because of the unintended consequences.

As I sit on the floor listening and braid strands of my hair, I think about what this means. I've never really thought about unintended consequences before. I guess things aren't always what they seem at face value. Trying to help doesn't mean you're actually helping. Dad moves on to the next ministry update letter, but I tuck this idea away.

U-TURN

What I learned as a child listening to Dad read about the slave-buying fiasco comes back to me as I work through what I've learned about drugs and addiction. Intent doesn't equal outcome, for one thing. But the second lesson, which I didn't even recognize until I was an adult, is equally as important. The organization admitted that a well-intended plan had failed, and they changed course. They could have kept going, giving their readers feel-good stories about the slaves they were freeing. The readers would've felt great and never known the unintended harm their contributions were causing, and the organization could likely have raised lots more money. Instead, they prioritized the truth of the outcome, and were humble enough to say, "We were wrong and we need to change course." Maybe this is the path forward with drugs.

A NEW SET OF LENSES

Drug policy wouldn't be the first time people or laws have been wrong. Every generation has blind spots, and history is littered with unhelpful and unjust laws that had to be fixed. State and federal elected officials today frequently change the law because there is agreement that the current laws still aren't perfect.

It's easy for us to look back on the blind spots of previous generations and say, "How could they not *see*?" It's a lot harder to wonder what our grandchildren will say about us a few decades from now. Will they look at the way we handle drugs and addiction today and shake their heads in disbelief at how long we continued failed policies? If we could take just a few steps back and look at the landscape of drug policy over the last 100 years, I think we see that what we know today about the causes of addiction and the best ways to reduce harm from drugs are not reflected in our laws. And what we know does not work is what we keep doing.

The thing about blind spots is that we can't see them. Without a posture of humility and curiosity, we all risk innocent ignorance or even incredible self-delusion. When our blind spots become visible, though, the best thing we can do is dig in and do the hard work of change.

Once I read the research on the causes of addiction, it was pretty easy to get behind not arresting people for possessing drugs. I may not agree with their drug use, and they may have an addiction that's destroying them and their families, but for most people, an arrest will compound problems, not solve them. It was easy to see that arresting Joanne would not help her or Beckham.

But undoing the broader collateral damage of crime and contamination that stem from prohibition would mean allowing drugs that are currently illegal to be brought back into some form of a legal market for adult use. Maybe tightly regulated through prescriptions or more loosely regulated through an age-to-purchase model as we have with alcohol and tobacco, but it's hard to get past the word "legal." Yikes. Trying to understand the complicated subject of drugs, addiction, and policy has felt a bit like zooming out to see the whole picture of a huge puzzle... then looking for a solution that addresses the big picture, not just one piece. The solution I've come to see is indeed allowing adults to make a broader range of choices about their drug use in a legal, regulated market. It took me by surprise, too. But the closer I look, there it is...staring me in the face. We can fix too many prescription opioids being handed out by cracking down, but then more people die from contaminated street drugs. We can give more people access to treatment, which is good, but the majority of people who use drugs aren't addicted to them. They don't need treatment, but they're still at risk of getting contaminated drugs and dying anyway. Only legal access helps solve the problem of unnecessary incarceration of consumers *and* the crime and contamination disaster.

The US has spent 100 years and over 1 trillion dollars trying to eliminate drug supply and drug demand largely by force. Yet we can't even keep drugs out of jails and prisons! The economic reality of supply and demand wins every time. We have tried to take a complex problem with nuanced solutions and turn it into a simple problem with easy solutions. Yet when we use the word "legal," genuine concern is a frequent response. James Moore, who lost his uncle and his son to the collateral damage of prohibition, now believes this concern is actually the opposite of what it should be. He says with passion, "Every fear that the person has for what would happen if there were legalization – every single fear – is already happening every single day in every community in our country. It's just happening in the worst possible way, with no protections in place, to the most vulnerable people." Death, disease, crime, addiction, broken families, devastated lives. Prohibition causes or incentivizes all of these, but it has gone on for so many decades that it feels like the natural state of things.

In reality, using the criminal justice system to address the use of substances was a radical new idea 100 years ago. Before that time, even drugs like heroin and cocaine were legal. If you developed an addiction, you were treated by your doctor. They could even prescribe you medical-grade heroin to keep you stable while you addressed the root causes of your addiction.

Ending drug prohibition, in a nutshell, is allowing adults to make a broader range of legal choices about their substance use. It would be less of an experiment than prohibition was when it started just over 100 years ago. A lot of us have just forgotten or never known that part of our country's history. Allowing legal access to drugs isn't a new idea, it's an old idea. One that seems increasingly wise. The term "legalization" should really be "re-legalization."

Our "drug war" was started based on theory, not evidence, and there aren't many people who say it has succeeded. By its own measures of success, it has failed in every way. Instead, we could move back to a health-centered approach to drugs, which is the opposite of the criminal justice approach we have now. When I tell people that I've been on a journey of changing my mind in favor of health-centered approaches to drugs and addiction, it resonates. There is almost universal agreement that healthy people is what we want. Most people recognize the criminal justice approach of the past decades hasn't worked and a health-centered approach might work better, but it's still a challenge to think through and embrace what that actually means.

At first glance, a legal, regulated market for drugs seems like a huge shift. Yet, if you look closely, the effort to ban drugs was a big shift, too. Yes, not arresting consumers would be a huge change for the criminal justice system, but it's more of a rewind than a revision of its role.

It seems like a big part of the challenge of change is that we haven't made the connection between the health-centered approach that might work better, and the policies and laws that bring it about.

A health-centered approach certainly has challenges, though. The medical community won't respond correctly to drug use or addiction every time, and consumers will still make some terrible choices just like they do now sometimes with alcohol and tobacco. But I would much rather entrust the health of people like Joanne and Jeffrey Moore to someone who spent years getting trained in healthcare and addiction treatment than to a police officer who doesn't have medical expertise. The criminal justice system is the right tool for some things, but it's not the right tool for a health issue.

Some form of legal access to drugs for adults and an evidence-based approach to addiction makes sense to me now when I look at the root causes of harm, but an avalanche of questions comes as my perspective shifts. Can I really support that as a Christian? As a conservative? As a mother? If jail isn't helpful for people struggling with addiction, what is? Are there other treatment options we haven't explored that could help far more people? And what do I actually *do* with everything I've learned?

The questions swirl as I turn a corner and begin weighing whether or not my deepest values are compatible with what seems like the most comprehensive, lasting solution to so many problems related to drugs. But they're swirling around a big elephant in the room that has to be dealt with first. Too many years have passed since most prohibited drugs were legal, and we've lost our cultural memory of that time. The memory we have now is Big Pharma and pill mills. How do I square the disaster of prohibition with the risks of legal drug sales?

CHAPTER 17

THE OTHER WAR

As the camera comes on, I see Will and Sarah Morgan sitting side-by-side on the couch in their living room. I'm surprised to see Sarah since I thought I was just hopping on a Zoom call with Will, an unfortunate necessity because COVID has shut everything down and we can't meet at a coffee shop. It's been 15 years since Will and I graduated from Belhaven University, and I haven't seen him since then. He's wearing a Jurassic Park t-shirt which makes me smile because when we were in college he wore a polo, khakis, and dress shoes every day. As an 18-year-old he dressed like college was his professional job. He interacted in class like it was too. He asked questions, challenged teachers, and engaged in spirited debate. I was a high achiever, but in college my goal wasn't to learn. It was to make great grades while having as much clean fun as possible. Will was there to learn. Even though our college was small and we had a lot of classes together, we didn't have the same circle of friends and after college we parted ways. I didn't know anything about Will's journey as a pain patient until he sent me a message on Facebook after I started sharing publicly what I was learning about drugs and addiction.

The experience he shares with me on our Zoom call over the next hour illustrates the plight of millions of patients on a new front of drug prohibition - the crackdown on access to *legal* opioids.

HUNTING FOR ANSWERS

Will lived a pretty normal life, graduating college the same year I did and marrying Sarah, a girl I always thought was one of the most beautiful women on campus. They were happily married and building an enjoyable life…with few major bumps in the road. Then, out of the blue, on a Sunday morning in September 2010, Will felt something pop in his groin area. No pain, just pressure and discomfort. Over the next several days it got worse. He went to the doctor but they couldn't find anything wrong. By the end of the week, though, he was in excruciating pain. Since that time, Will and Sarah have been on a journey of doctors, acupuncture, supplements, special pillows, experimental surgeries, traveling to other states for novel treatments, emergency rooms, and so many medications. So many opioids. After several years, one doctor finally diagnosed the source of pain as the pudendal nerve, and the onset, as well as the flair-ups, seem to be triggered by stress. But those answers of origin didn't fix the pain.

Will always had a high tolerance for pain. Growing up, he broke bones, had surgeries, and never asked for more pain medication. When he broke his ankle in college, the doctor cast his foot so tightly that it cut off the circulation in his pinkie toe. It hurt, but he pushed through, never calling the doctor. When the cast came off, the toe was black. The doctor asked him why on earth he hadn't told them about the pain in his toe. "I just dealt with it," was Will's response. It hadn't occurred to him to complain about it. But the pain he was experiencing now was of a different kind. One of the less graphic ways he described it to me was like sitting on a balloon filled with razor blades and fire. "It really was like being tortured all the time. It was horrible," Will remembers. Even telling me about his journey is difficult for him, which is why he asked Sarah to sit with him on our Zoom call. He needed her support just to get through retelling the story.

Through these years, there were times when the pain medication his doctor was willing to give him was enough so he could function. Other times, even strong opioids weren't enough to take the edge off. Unfortunately for Will, his pain journey started around the same time doctors were being encouraged to cut down on prescribing opioids. Over the next several years some states turned those guidelines into laws, and the Drug Enforcement Agency (DEA) began arresting doctors they decided were prescribing too many opioids. For pain patients like Will, it ushered in a new era of suffering. Doctors were increasingly unwilling to give him the opioids he needed to control the pain. When Will needed a medical excuse for work when he took a week off because the pain left him incapacitated, his doctor asked him if it was really that bad that he couldn't work. Will faced the same suspicions over and over again. Some doctors believed him. They could see he was in debilitating pain. Others thought he was just an addict faking it to get his next fix of opioids. "It wasn't an issue of wanting to get high, it was an issue of wanting the pain to stop," Will explains. "My life revolved around this medication, but everything I did was to try to get *off* this pain medication. That's why I did all the treatments, all the alternative therapies."

Even though Will and Sarah were overjoyed to welcome one son and have another on the way, their marriage was under immense strain as Will tried to help people understand how much physical pain he was in, and Sarah was told that if Will took any more opioids he could overdose and die. But, honestly, death was beginning to sound like the only way out of the hell Will was living every day.

As doctors stopped returning his phone calls and his access to opioids became more and more sporadic, he felt like he only had two options. He could start buying drugs illegally or commit suicide. He simply could not stay alive and live with this much pain.

True to his straight-laced roots, he didn't have the first clue how to buy a drug off the street, so that left him with suicide as the only option in his mind. He'd heard that if you shoot yourself in the heart, you won't bleed as much. He even thought about the brick wall on the side of their house he could stand against as he pulled the trigger. Maybe that would make the least amount of mess, he decided. Even though the rest of his life was wonderful, Will was edging toward a cliff. "I've got a 4-year-old kid and another on the way. I have a good job. I work from home," Will remembers with desperation in his voice. "Everything was great except I was in an enormous amount of pain. Because of the way the law is now, I couldn't get the treatment I needed."

After one of his pain management doctors refused to treat him anymore, Will went to the Emergency Room for help. The doctors in the ER told him sympathetically that it was a terrible time to be in pain. "Everyone was too terrified to treat me," Will says in exasperation. What were they afraid of? Getting arrested. Instead of doctors being able to make the best decisions for their patients, it's now enforcement authorities who decide what is appropriate for doctors to prescribe. "I think we need doctors to be making these decisions, not law enforcement professionals," says Will. "I've heard from doctors that they would treat pain differently if they could." But most are concerned about the federal DEA. "The pain management doctor who eventually cut me off, he told me 'If it comes to helping you or keeping my medical license, I'm keeping my medical license,'" Will remembers. "The doctors say they know they're not treating pain, they know people need help, but they're not making the decisions. Law enforcement is."

The war on illegal opioids has been extended to a war on legal opioids. Millions of pain patients like Will are caught in the middle, with the option to live with the pain, end their life, or buy their opioids on the underground market. The DEA can stop doctors from prescribing, but the guy on the corner will always be welcoming new clients. In fact, he's tickled pink that legal opioids are harder and harder to get. The wrong people are winning here.

LIGHT IN THE DARKNESS

In the last few years, Will found a doctor who understood his pain. He also was convinced that the opioids that used to alleviate pain for Will were actually causing pain now. They developed a plan to move Will to a different, lower-dose opioid. He'd tried it already, years ago, and it hadn't worked. But now it did. Pain management is complicated, kind of like addiction is. Every person is different. Every medication affects them differently. And the same medication or treatment may work in one season of life when it didn't previously. Will sees both sides of the opioid conversation. "Not treating pain is not an option," says Will emphatically. "But on the other hand, I'm the poster child for opioids eventually causing pain. I'm also the poster child for opioids not stopping pain. If opioids were enough to fix my pain problem, my problem would've been gone."

Will still has pain every day, but it's usually only a fraction of what it was. He lives in constant fear of his insurance changing which medications they cover, or of a flare-up persisting. The question of whether or not he'll have access to medication when he needs it is always floating in the back of his mind. "Maybe we need to treat people as individuals. Maybe we shouldn't have a grand federal plan to treat pain," Will offers. "People aren't all alike." The people best positioned to determine appropriate treatment are doctors, though, not police officers. It makes no sense that doctors have to attend years of medical school before they can treat a patient with opioids, but law enforcement agencies with no medical training then determine if the doctor is treating a patient properly. Medical boards can hold doctors accountable. They're the ones who have the expertise to determine if a doctor is practicing with disregard for the patient's best interests. They can discipline or revoke licenses when necessary.

IT'S NOT ALL OR NOTHING

The issue of prescription opioids is a really hard issue for many people who watched large pharmaceutical companies aggressively market them. Where there was criminal activity, it should be prosecuted. But at the same time, a response that causes millions of pain patients to suffer is not winning. Driving droves of people to the underground market where they're buying contaminated substances and are far more likely to die is not winning. We can hold companies accountable for criminal activity and still allow consumers to legally access the drugs they need.

Sometimes I think we forget that opioids are nothing short of a miracle drug. They've eased pain and suffering and improved the quality of life for millions of people. For the vast majority of people who use opioids, their use never turns problematic. And for the people who do become addicted, do we want them under the care of a doctor or a drug dealer? A few doctors operate like drug dealers, but that's no reason to send everyone to a dealer on the street. That's a reaction, not a solution. The vast majority of doctors perform their jobs with expertise and care.

With drugs, we never get the option of "perfect." We are broken people, in a broken world, with potentially harmful substances. We have to weigh the pros and cons. Legal opioids have pros and cons. Illicit opioids only have the latter. Pushing people away from medical professionals and toward professional criminals is a policy disaster. Our neighbors who are pain patients like Will are paying a heavy price, and so are all of the people dying from contamination because there is no legal access to the drug they want to use.

Every policy has trade-offs. We've traded an abundance of opioid prescriptions for an abundance of graves. There needs to be a middle ground. If we don't pursue a path that allows people to legally access drugs they want or need, we will inevitably minimize opioids but maximize suffering and death.

Even though I have concerns about the harm that will still be present when we move more drugs into legal markets for adults, I'm convinced now that the trade-offs are worth it times ten. Even though legal access does not mean we will incentivize or encourage drug use, there will still be significant problems. We won't find a perfect path, but it will be a better path that gives more people an opportunity to live out their full potential as image-bearers of God. Could that path actually work in practice, though?

CHAPTER 18

NUTS AND BOLTS

Thomas, my husband, walked into the grocery store, strolled past the produce, dry goods, frozen foods, and snack aisles. All the way on the other end of the store he took a left and stopped in front of the beer. He only drinks about a can per week, so a case lasts for a couple months. In front of him were a wealth of options in open cases. He picked out some Blue Moon, walked back to the checkout, showed his ID to confirm his age, and paid. That was it, and he walked out of the store with a legal drug. A drug that can impair you and even kill you.

As I try to envision what adult access to more drugs might look like in the real world, it helps me to realize that we already have numerous regulatory structures for various legal drugs today.

Some drugs are sold over the counter with no age restrictions, like ibuprofen. There are also pharmacy models (think pseudoephedrine), age-to-purchase models (like alcohol), licensed premises models (the local bar), and prescription models (like opioids).

One of these regulatory frameworks could be used for a particular drug coming back into the legal market, or we could develop new ones based on the particular risk factors of each drug. Most states that have made cannabis legal have developed new regulations specific to that plant, although some states have definitely done it better than others. As in underground markets, customers are ultimately in control. This can be very challenging for states; if taxes are too high or regulations are too tight, consumers won't switch to buying legally. This is a huge problem in a number of states that have legalized cannabis for adult use. But the problem isn't with legalization, it's with overregulation and taxation.

If the goal is to bankrupt the underground market and get people to stop using contaminated drugs, legal access has to be viable and competitive with the underground market. Legal access by law–but not in practice–won't solve anything.

In addition to regulatory frameworks on the consumer side, there are ways to protect the broader community too. As with alcohol, being able to buy it doesn't give adults the right to endanger others by drinking and driving or drinking and assaulting someone. Shifting away from prohibition doesn't mean shifting away from accountability. Similar to our approach to alcohol, we need to hold adults accountable for how their drug use affects others. A healthy society is not a lawless one. For instance, if a person engages in theft, they should be arrested — even if the root cause is an addiction they're trying to pay for.

This scenario is where drug courts might be most helpful. They can provide accountability and justice after a legitimate crime while also addressing the core problem.

A pendulum swing from one extreme of arresting people for minor drug infractions to another extreme of letting people engage in any behavior they want without consequence is profoundly harmful to the whole community. As with almost everything in life, extremes are unhelpful, and solutions lie on a nuanced path between.

Changing our laws around drug production and consumption wouldn't change our laws about theft or assault or any number of other crimes people might engage in whether they're using drugs or not. Instead, it would actually free up law enforcement to spend more time solving crime, which is important because today almost half of all violent crimes are never solved.[4] Our officers and our citizens would be better served by redirecting time and funds to pursuing justice for these victims. So what would legal access to more drugs look like in the real world?

THE REAL WORLD

A first step to curb overdose could be allowing doctors to prescribe opioids to people who are addicted to them, instead of cutting them off immediately. Again, we don't get to wave a magic wand and just make people's addictions go away. The choice for millions of people is pure opioids from a doctor or contaminated ones on the street. If staying alive is the first big goal, opening a legal pathway so people don't use contaminated drugs is crucial.

Longer term we could consider the best way to allow adults to purchase a broader range of naturally-occurring stimulants and depressants legally...such as smokable opium and coca leaves. These options can provide alternatives to much riskier drugs and keep people safer. The challenges of legally regulating riskier drugs are much greater, but I can't see how anyone is safer by forcing powerful drugs into the free-for-all of the underground market.

The scary reality we have to keep in front of us is that the riskiest drugs can already be bought with the tap of a phone screen by kids and adults alike in just about every town in this country. The question of access has already been answered, but we can still influence the who, what, and where questions.

In addition to workable regulations, our culture would simultaneously need to develop new and healthy social norms in order to shift a drug out of the underground and back into legal access. Unfortunately, we've pushed so many drugs into the shadows for so long that the process of developing social norms as we have around alcohol and tobacco will take time and will certainly be painful. Now let me be clear, thinking about legal access to some drugs definitely makes me uncomfortable, but the cost of comfort is too high now. If we want solutions that work, we're going to have to get a little uncomfortable. It will be a painful process to reverse failed policy, but right now we're on a painful path to nowhere. If we have to experience pain, it would be nice if it was at least in service of a healthier future.

One of my biggest fears with legal access to more drugs is that more people will use them. This seems very likely to me, even though most of us have absolutely no interest in trying cocaine or heroin, even if they were legal. But still, surely there are some people who are deterred by the law. The history of alcohol prohibition and re-legalization is helpful to remember related to this concern too. After alcohol was re-legalized, consumption levels did increase, but then they stabilized and are *below pre-prohibition levels*, 100 years later.[5] If our history with alcohol and tobacco, two of the most harmful drugs on the planet, is that their use has a ceiling and is also able to be significantly influenced by regulations and social norms, it's not a stretch to believe we would have a similar experience with other drugs.

For some of us, it's easier to get on board with making something like marijuana legal again because the risk profile is comparatively low. But when we talk about drugs with higher risk profiles like heroin and cocaine, the hesitations multiply. But think of it this way: the more potentially risky a drug is, the more reason there is to have some control over it. People aren't dying from marijuana overdose. They're dying from cocaine, opioid, and methamphetamine overdose. There are very real and wise concerns about legal access to riskier drugs, but prohibition doesn't have good answers to those concerns. Making a drug legal at least gives us some control over who produces it, what ingredients are in it, and who buys it. Prohibition strips all of that away.

James Moore still has a cut-and-dried view of the world, just like he did as a zealous law enforcement officer getting drugs off the streets. But it's a different view now. "Would you rather live in a society where deaths are prevalent and the substance is illegal, or would you rather live in a society where the substance is legal and regulated and deaths are minimized?" he asks. "Because that's the choice." His son Jeffrey was never arrested during the 10 years of his addiction. He never felt the sting of the criminal justice system as a consumer. But the outcome of prohibition—contamination—still found him. James hopes his loss can help others see how to prevent their own. "If everyone had to realize the very real possibility of losing their loved one as a choice," he says soberly, "some of the ideas they might think are undoable or revolutionary now will start to look mighty appealing."

CHOOSING WHO PROFITS

Along with the concern that more people will use drugs if they're legal, a lot of people I've talked to don't want businesses making money off of drug use, especially if that use becomes an addiction. The idea that a company can manufacture a drug and make money off selling it is profoundly disturbing to a lot of people who lived through the last 20 years. That's very understandable, but we don't get the choice of whether drugs are sold. We get to decide who sells them. Would we rather have cartels and gangs make money from selling them, or legal businesses? We might be uncomfortable with the idea that anyone is making money off of drugs, but somebody is. Consumers are paying. The choice is who they're paying. Good regulations can help avoid some of the pitfalls of our history with opioids, but we have to face the reality that someone will always make money when drugs are sold.

Like I said, it still makes me uncomfortable when I think about adults having legal access to more drugs. When I see marijuana dispensaries that celebrate the "stoner" vibe, I cringe. When I'm walking through a city and smell marijuana, I automatically have negative feelings.

I don't like some of the tradeoffs of legal access to marijuana, for instance, but I'm still convinced it's the best path to significantly reduce global harm related to cannabis. When we think about tradeoffs, it's important to note that almost every problem that comes with legal access is also a problem under prohibition, plus some. For instance, are there corrupt regulators in the cannabis industry? Even if there are, there are no regulators in the underground industry. Do some cannabis dispensaries sell to minors? I'm sure some do, but everyone sells to minors in the illegal market. Some cannabis tax dollars aren't spent wisely, but the underground market has no tax dollars to spend at all. We'll always have problems with drugs, but we don't have to add the problems of prohibition.

INVESTMENT AVERSION

As I began to reckon with these conclusions, I still felt something inside myself that I've seen crop up over and over as I've talked to people about what I learned. When someone has a personal or professional investment of some kind in a certain idea being right, it's exponentially harder to consider if it's not. I started calling it "investment aversion" and even included a slide at the beginning of my presentations to explain that the more impacted your life will be by changing how we approach drugs, the harder it is to be open to the idea. I encouraged people to recognize this aversion for what it is and try to overcome it and be curious anyway. Later a friend told me that what I observed and called investment aversion is very close to the idea of confirmation bias. Confirmation bias is the tendency we all have to accept information that confirms what we already believe and discard new information that challenges it, even if the new information is true. It has been observed, written about and studied for hundreds of years. Remember, my degree is in Bible, not psychology. To give a biblical phrase to my introduction to confirmation bias, "There is nothing new under the sun."[6]

I see it everywhere now, including in my own life. For me as a foster mom, I tried to discard the reality that Joanne is a mom like me. The situation was easier for me if she wasn't. Dr. Alexander's fellow academics didn't want the results of Rat Park to be true because their careers would be impacted by it. Parents who called the police on their child in an attempt to force them to stop using drugs might find it very hard to accept the idea that incarceration could have made the problem worse.

Companies that supply products and services to the prison industry have a financial aversion to shifting away from corralling so many people into prison cells. Addiction treatment centers that get patients through court orders after people get arrested for drug possession will likely struggle to be open to changing that approach because their business model will be impacted. The more it will cost us - emotionally, professionally, financially, etc. - the harder it is to rethink something. I don't see that as greed or carelessness as much as it's just human nature. Once we're aware of it, we can get curious about whether new information is actually false, or whether its truth is just making us uncomfortable.

Police officers who have spent their careers enforcing our current drug laws and have lost fellow officers to that cause understandably tend to have the hardest time rethinking them. It seems strange and unfair to me that society looks to law enforcement to tell us whether we need to chart a new course with drugs when law enforcement has invested more time, money, and lives than almost anyone else in the current approach. It's like asking a doctor if the surgery he's been performing for 30 years has actually been harmful to his patients. Even if it undeniably has been, how can he be expected to give an unbiased assessment?

Changing our minds is hard. Changing them when we've invested personally, professionally, or financially in a particular perspective requires deep courage. Sometimes the cost is almost too much to bear.

James Moore is able to hold several things in tension that I think are important, especially as we think about the people we've put on the front lines of prohibition. James is proud of his service as a police officer and he supports and respects his friends in law enforcement today. But he also believes our laws have given those officers an impossible and ultimately harmful task. The sooner we shift resources and responsibilities to activities that truly make communities safer, the better off everyone will be.

I may not have the same experiences or investments that James resonates with, but I have three that still feel pretty big. Even if legal access can solve a lot of the drug-related problems we have today, can I support it as a Christian, as a mother, and as a conservative? My commitment to my Christian identity started young.

CHAPTER 19

FAITH AND VALUES

Thank goodness Mississippi is far away from that godless place, I thought.

About two miles west of Loden Place is an apartment complex where a lot of seminary students live, and I babysit for the families sometimes. Today I've just finished a babysitting job and overhear an adult mention that California just made marijuana legal. I'm thirteen and have never seen or even smelled marijuana. I'm not exactly sure what it is even, but it's clear from the conversation that it's a drug, it's bad, and California is clearly a pagan place. I settle into the back seat for the car ride home and feel relieved. Mississippi has morals and values. We would never do something crazy like that. I never expected another Mississippian to challenge me on it fifteen years later.

Out of the blue, a fellow conservative Christian asked me if I thought drugs should be legal for adult use instead of criminalized. This was several years before I met Joanne and it only took a split-second for my heart to start racing and my blood pressure to shoot through the roof. How could they ask me that?! I am a Christian. I am conservative. They didn't say it, but what I heard was, "Do you want people to destroy their lives?" "Do you think we should celebrate drugs?" "Do you want to give up your values?" I was so angry I left the room. Even having the conversation felt like it would lend legitimacy to an insane idea. They raised the question with curiosity instead of the disdain it deserved, and all I heard was a challenge to a long-held belief. From someone in my tribe!

Until I met Joanne and felt the beating hearts caught up in the question, I had zero interest in rethinking how we approach drugs and addiction. Now I've been swimming in the deep end of addiction, drugs, and policy for over a year, learning as much as I can between calling out spelling words to my sons and recruiting volunteers for a church ministry I lead. From the beginning it was clear that if we're even a little bit wrong in the way we approach drugs, the impact of that error is seismic. That's what keeps me learning. If there is a better way to reduce harm, it will impact millions of people every day.

I've become convinced that making more drugs legal for adult use - like alcohol and tobacco already are - is the best way to reduce harm pragmatically. But my commitments as a Christian, a mother, and a conservative run deep. Is this policy shift compatible with my morals and values?

MORALITY

When I was first asked what I thought about making more drugs legal for adults, my intense reaction was triggered by the feeling that moral ground was on the line. I thought drug use was immoral, so it should be illegal. Making it legal would signal that it was no big deal. As I think about the practical impacts of prohibition, the moral and legal questions begin to separate from one another in my mind.

For most of my life, I thought using drugs crossed a moral line, even a sinful one. But just like my experiences of suffering earlier in my life softened the lines of my rigid way of viewing the world, what I learn about drugs helps me see a lot of nuances I've missed before. Tylenol and Advil are drugs, and they change the way I feel. I don't think using them is wrong. Even with stronger drugs like opioids, there's a lot of gray area. When I had abdominal surgery a few years ago, I took opioids and that wasn't sinful or harmful. It was actually helpful. There are legitimate reasons to change the way we physically feel, changes that improve our lives. What about emotional changes? It's not a problem that people take medication for mental health challenges like anxiety, depression, or bipolar disorder. I would be one of the first people to encourage someone to explore all mental health options that could help them thrive. As I've learned, it's gotten a lot harder to label drug use in general as "wrong" when so much of it clearly isn't. Maybe using drugs for pleasure is where the line falls for me.

But even there, the lines get very gray, very quickly. Coffee is a mild drug, but Christians, conservatives, and mothers like me drink it for pleasure every day. Alcohol is a much stronger drug, but many people from those same groups drink small amounts of it for pleasure regularly. The Bible certainly forbids drunkenness, but it doesn't speak against moderate use of alcohol. It even encourages it in 1 Timothy 5:23, and in John 2 Jesus himself turns water into wine at a wedding.

Mulling over the question of sin and drug use, I've read articles by Christian authors who make the case that the recreational use of alcohol is okay because it doesn't cloud your thinking, but marijuana or opioids do. They draw the line at brain impact and clear thinking. But this seems divorced from the realities of alcohol. No one in the history of the world has ever ingested alcohol without feeling its impact as a depressant. It's a mild poison that immediately slows your brain function and thought process. If you only drink a little, the impact is minimal. If you drink a lot, the impact is significant. Some people certainly enjoy the taste of alcohol, but the taste is always combined with the effect. The relaxation a beer offers after a stressful day of work doesn't come from the taste. It comes from the chemical impact as a depressant slows brain function. There's definitely a sinful line on the continuum of alcohol use, and I presume the same is true with other drugs. The line is just a lot harder to draw than I first thought.

FAITH

However, even as I continue to ponder the moral question, I realize I don't need a definitive answer before tackling the legal question. Even if there are forms of drug use that are immoral or even sinful, that doesn't necessarily mean they should be illegal. The Ten Commandments helped me see why.

Christians are unified in the belief that breaking any of the Ten Commandments is by definition sinful. There are no gray lines here (finally!). But only two of the commandments - murder and theft - are criminalized today by law. Christians aren't lobbying to put everyone who breaks the Sabbath in jail or to make it illegal to covet someone else's new boat. We don't even put people in prison for adultery, even though it's a horrible assault on one of the most hallowed institutions of the Christian faith. There are times when religious convictions and the appropriate role of government to protect its citizens overlap, as with murder and theft. My pro-life values fit into this overlapping category, but Christians generally agree that most immoral or sinful behavior should not be punished with jail time. Criminally prosecuting anyone who breaks the Ten Commandments would be a gross misuse of government power and a recipe for disaster.

I had never consciously thought through the differences between religious conviction and law before, but the flipside was immediately obvious. Using civil or criminal law to set our moral compass isn't wise. Christians don't look at the law and decide that pornography or infidelity is acceptable just because it isn't criminal. The law can set guard rails on our behavior in society, but it can't tell us how to follow God or even how to love our neighbor. Similarly, religious conviction and even virtuous ideals shouldn't be enforced through the law. If they are, they lose their meaning and transformational power, becoming not much more than coerced behavior modification. The question of whether drug use is right or wrong is a different question than whether it should be legal or not. As I recognize the distinction between virtue and law, I'm convinced that my Christian values aren't in conflict with the idea of ending drug prohibition. What about my other values?

CONSERVATIVE VALUES

My identity is in being a follower of Jesus, but I consider myself a conservative too. Now the challenge is sorting out whether or not my new viewpoints are compatible with my conservative values. This one is a lot easier as I learn about the cause-and-effect nature of prohibition and realize how much I have simply misunderstood it. It seems to me now that sensibly regulating a wider range of drugs for legal adult use is much more compatible with values like limited government, fiscal responsibility, personal responsibility, employment opportunity, strong families, safe communities, and the sanctity of life. I'm not a conservative who is shifting toward a progressive approach to drugs. I'm a conservative that sees leaving prohibition behind us as a return to a conservative approach to drugs.

As I sorted through my conservative values, one of the biggest hurdles was considering whether prohibition is still helpful as a warning signal, even if the practical outcomes are terrible. I'm still hesitant about the cultural response to removing the stamp of "Illegal" on some drugs. Even though there seem to be an awful lot of people who don't care how the government categorizes drugs, certainly *some* people are deterred from using them because they are illegal. So it seems likely that more people will use drugs if they're legal, and there's a real risk that we swing from one extreme of prohibition and incarceration to another extreme of celebrating drug use and being stoned. That wouldn't be good, but it's crucial to remember that levels of drug use are only one indicator of effective policy. It's one patch of trees on our hike up the mountain. We have to see the panoramic view from the top and consider the myriad other outcomes of a policy to see if it's effective. That would include rates of addiction, overdose, death, disease, crime, family stability, economic impact, etc. *All outcomes*, not just one or two, have to be included if we're going to be serious about evaluating policy success.

Even though the law might be an effective warning signal for some people, we've seen with tobacco that there are much more effective ways to combat drug use on a large scale. We know that we can effectively send a social message without prohibition and criminalization.

As I think through all of this, it seems to me that ending prohibition is more compatible with my moral, religious, and political beliefs than continuing down that path, but I also have a house full of sons. Is a world where drugs are legal for adults really the world I want my boys to live in?

CHAPTER 20

OUR KIDS

The blue walls of my bedroom reflect the late afternoon light as it slants in through the window that faces west. A couple of weeks ago I got up my nerve and wrote another opinion article and submitted it to Mississippi's statewide newspaper. It was printed today. The nerves that coursed through my body a year ago when I wrote the first one and met James Moore aren't as strong today. I feel a little more confident. A few emails trickle in from readers since I decided to keep my email address on the bio line. It connected me with James last time, so it's worth the risk of getting some angry responses too. One of the replies launches me into a phone call with a mother whose daughter has struggled with heroin addiction for years. As I walk back and forth in front of the bed, the woman shares how her family has been through hell, spending tens of thousands of dollars on treatment for their daughter, bailing her out of jail, and eventually cutting her out of their life entirely.

My kids are still young, but I can't help but wonder what this journey has been like for her as a mother. She and her husband have successful careers and gave their daughter everything they could growing up. What happened? The anger in her voice isn't veiled. The heartbreak behind it streams through the phone as we talk, me trying to understand her experience and her trying to work through whether there are better solutions like the ones in my article. There is no resolution, though. Their family is still in shreds, and the ideas in the article about what could help families like theirs aren't implemented yet. We say goodbye as two mothers who love their children dearly and want what's best for them. How can we keep our kids safer, reducing the risk that more families experience what this mother and her family are going through?

Following in my footsteps won't always be a good idea for my boys, but I hope my experience with drugs in my youth is theirs - nonexistent. Protecting their developing brains is so important. Certainly banning a drug will discourage some kids from trying it in the first place, but it can also backfire by sparking the interest of others. Teenagers tend to be drawn toward "forbidden fruit." I still feel the tug of trying to force my kids not to use drugs, though, and leveraging the law in the hope that it will deter them can feel mighty tempting. But the reality is kids can learn about and order illegal drugs on the internet in about five seconds. Just because I don't know how to do that doesn't mean they don't. Abstinence by force is a complete illusion, much to the dismay of many of us parents.

I wonder if honest education and open conversations might get us much further in helping our kids understand drugs and the very real risks of using them. I was in my early 30s before I learned that some drugs are depressants and others are stimulants. Similarly, understanding how too much of a depressant or stimulant causes overdose, and why mixing drugs exponentially increases risk, didn't happen until after I met Joanne and got curious. Our kids need a much more robust knowledge bank about drugs and what causes risk. Their world is awash in opportunities to access a kaleidoscope of drugs with one tap of a phone screen or one conversation in the hallway at school. One mother I talked to homeschooled her children, but her son was introduced to marijuana through kids in the church youth group, just like Joanne was. Drugs are everywhere.

An approach of honest education has done wonders in shifting choices around cigarette smoking over the last 50 years. It may strengthen our kids' internal resolve to make healthy choices today, which is the very best way we can prevent drug use. We can't force our kids to make wise choices, but we can empower them to. Honest education, not a law, is the best way to help kids say no to drugs. Alcohol and tobacco use by teens is at its lowest point in decades because of regulations and social norms[7], not prohibition. But if they go against wisdom and experiment anyway, making drugs legal for adult use may actually save their lives.

EVEN IF

If my boys choose to go against what my husband and I are teaching them and use drugs, the very first thing we want is to make sure they don't die. Unfortunately, death is much more likely if the drugs they get their hands on were produced on the underground market. The same potency and purity issues killing adults who use street drugs are also killing our kids. For youth who drink alcohol underage today, it's certainly not healthy and we should do everything we can to prevent it. But at least the alcohol they get has been regulated for purity and labeled for potency. We know there's no rat poison or brick dust or fentanyl in it. Not so with drugs sold on the street. As long as the underground market thrives, our kids are much more likely to get contaminated drugs, even if they don't realize it.

I also want my boys to have a harder time getting drugs, so I want age restrictions on purchasing them. No one on a street corner is checking ID. Age-to-purchase restrictions as we have for alcohol are no guarantee that youth won't get their hands on it. But at least it creates one barrier. The underground market has none. A 14-year-old can get heroin today just as easily as a 34-year-old. Numerous people have told me it was easier for them to get marijuana when they were in high school than alcohol, even though marijuana was illegal for everyone then, not just youth. That's because legal businesses have a financial incentive not to sell to kids so they don't lose their license to sell to the much larger adult market. Illegal businesses have a financial incentive to do the exact opposite. A customer is a customer, no matter how young. They're taking the same risk to sell to kids as they are to adults. Why discriminate?

Banning a drug provides no protection for our kids. Making it legal for adults at least puts up a few barriers and ensures that even if kids get their hands on it, it can be dosed appropriately and isn't contaminated.

Beyond keeping them alive and healthy, it seems obvious that the last thing I want for my sons is a criminal record. If it's clear that my own loved ones wouldn't benefit from having their employment opportunities permanently crippled, it's hard to make a case that other people's loved ones would somehow be better off with one. If one of my boys uses drugs or develops an addiction, I want them to have the widest door to help, not handcuffs.

Learning about what causes addiction hasn't made me less worried that my own kids might struggle. If anything, it has helped me see just how easily it can develop because of how broken and painful our world is. It doesn't mean our parenting failed, and it doesn't mean our kids are terrible. It's an indication that the hurt of a fallen world in all its array has found a place to set up camp in their hearts. That can happen even with a happy childhood and a loving family. Maybe the best way we can help our kids is by having honest conversations with them about drugs, teaching them healthy coping skills for the pain in their lives, and modeling how to seek professional help when it's needed. These are more effective tools to protect our kids from drug use or addiction than any law is anyway.

Each new thing I learned answered one of my questions and slowly convinced me that a step-by-step return of drugs to their rightful place as a health issue isn't just the best way to reduce harm, it's compatible with my deepest values. But even if we successfully moved all drugs back into legal, regulated markets and stopped arresting people for possessing drugs, we're still going to have to address addiction. Even the best policies won't solve it. So whether or not the laws of prohibition change, what can we do as families, friends, and communities to give people a better chance to avoid addiction in the first place, and stay alive, find hope, and recover if they do develop it?

CHAPTER 21

STAIR STEPS TO RECOVERY

"When I started to realize I was wrong about everything, Chance was 15 years old," Christi Berrong-Barber tells me as I settle in for the story. Her own learning journey and mine collided, just like James Moore's and mine did, and what she learned as the mother of someone struggling with addiction might shine some light on a better way to approach it.

Christi was at home taking care of her aunt who had serious medical needs. She'd been trying to get in touch with her son, Chance, all morning. He was out with a friend Christi wasn't crazy about, and now he wasn't answering his phone. As Christi finished the medical routine for her aunt's care, the phone rang. She had a sinking feeling in her gut. "I guess intuitively I knew something was wrong," she says. It was her sister, telling Christi a friend of hers had just called. Everyone knew everyone in their small Mississippi town, and the woman recognized Chance as she drove past him. The next words got all jumbled together for Christi as she tried to process what her sister was telling her. He's on the side of the road. Handcuffs. Arrested. Christi jumped in her car and tore down the street to see what on earth was going on. Several deputies' cars came into view. After parking, Christi tried to get to Chance as a female officer told her she couldn't be there. "That's my son!" Christi said, trying to be respectful while fighting panic. "I'll never forget seeing my son in the back of that police car." Chance and his friend had been caught injecting heroin in a convenience store parking lot.

Christi is a medical office manager. She's a strong woman, but less than 2 minutes into sharing her story with me, her voice breaks. Before this incident, she had no idea Chance had ever used *any* drug. *Injecting heroin?* "I had no clue how to deal with it," she remembers.

DOORKNOBS

As a child, Chance loved to read, was smart as a whip, and had an insatiable curiosity about the world around him. When he was in second grade he took the doorknobs off all the doors in the house just because he wanted to know how they worked. Why had he taken them all off, Christi asked in exasperation when she discovered the deed. "Because one of them might have worked differently, Mom," Chance responded innocently.

Christi laughs with joy as she tells me stories of her only child's early years. Her delight in her son is overflowing.

By middle school Chance was bored in class and started getting in trouble, so she homeschooled him and he did very well. But after a growth spurt made him a 6'3" 257-pound 14-year-old, he wanted to play football. She put him in private school, but it didn't shield him from exposure to drugs.

The months after Chance's first arrest were a steep learning curve for Christi. She learned, "My son could walk out of our house on a family farm in a town I had been born and raised in, in small-town Mississippi, and he could buy heroin. Easily."

Chance was able to graduate at sixteen years old from high school even as his addiction progressed, but within two years his life was ravaged by it. "We ran from one side of the country to the next chasing him," Christi remembers. She labels it the worst year of her life, buying bus tickets home for him more times than she can remember. As Chance's addiction deepened, Christi's goals shifted. Instead of every morning starting with the goal that she could change his life that day, her goal became to simply keep him alive. "That became my motto, I guess," she says. "Just keep him alive one more day. Maybe tomorrow he will want to get help."

(Christi with Chance at high school graduation)

As she told me the story, an image of a staircase popped into my mind. Most responses to drug addiction seem to view active addiction as the bottom of a staircase and total abstinence as the top. All the stairs in between are knocked out, and the goal is to jump from addiction to abstinence overnight. Once you've made the quantum leap and are abstinent, then you take one step at a time to build a thriving life. This approach has dominated addiction treatment for decades, and it does work for some people. But the vast majority of people who try abstinence will relapse. What happens then?

There was a time when relapse meant you just went back to that bottom step and took another leap at the top. For some drugs, like alcohol, you may get lots of tries. But for thousands of people taking the quantum leap when they're struggling with opioid addiction, relapse isn't leading back to the bottom step. It's leading to the funeral home.

OPIOID ADDICTION

When a person uses opioids for a period of time, the body becomes physically dependent on them and begins to build tolerance. The longer the person uses, the higher his or her tolerance gets. When people stop using, their body's tolerance falls, but they don't know how much. The same amount of opioids that used to get them high can now kill them. This is the scenario millions of people find themselves in. Attempted abstinence. Decreased tolerance. Relapse. And for thousands of them, that relapse is a death sentence. Drug use is risky, but a period of abstinence makes it even riskier.

Instead of viewing successful recovery as an overnight risky leap to abstinence, what if we viewed it as a journey toward a thriving life, celebrating one step at a time, whether the person is abstinent or not? It would encourage people to pursue a meaningful life rather than focusing so much on the drug they're using to fill the void.

It's important to acknowledge that the vast majority of people who use drugs - legal or illegal - don't develop an addiction. They use drugs occasionally but never meet the criteria for physical dependence or substance use disorder. That means that *the majority of people who use drugs don't need an intervention or treatment.* Sending them would be pointless and waste valuable beds. It would be like sending someone to treatment for alcoholism who has a glass of wine after work or a couple of beers when they're out with friends on a Friday night. The best way to reduce harm to most people who use drugs is to make sure they don't get arrested and don't die from contamination.

But for the minority of people whose drug use turns problematic, what if we built all the steps back into the staircase, so people could work toward a thriving life one step at a time as they built a personalized staircase to recovery? Instead of making people give up their coping mechanism *before* they have a life they want to be fully present for, why don't we encourage them to take a small step toward building it? That small step might be simply staying alive by using fentanyl testing strips or having the opioid overdose reversal medication naloxone on hand. When 100,000 people are dying every year from an overdose in the US, staying alive is a crucial first step. People shouldn't have to die to exit addiction.

If they can stay alive, they might become open to another step like seeing a doctor if they need medication, finding stable housing, or even just calling to check in and let a loved one know they're ok each day. For someone who's living on the street, their first steps will probably look very different from a doctor who's hiding his addiction but maintaining his job. Each person's journey into addiction is different. Each person's recovery journey will be too.

It might sound ridiculous to focus on small steps, like it just prolongs the problem. Our culture's focus on getting people into in-patient treatment for addiction at all costs has given us the idea that every person addicted must go to treatment if they're ever going to stop using drugs. But it's just not true.

PAYTON'S CLIMB

Payton, the boy who watched the tail lights on his mom's U-Haul trailer out his bedroom window as she abandoned him as a 13-year-old, is a good example. He hated knowing that he was addicted to opioids, but now he couldn't stop taking them or he'd be physically sick from withdrawal symptoms. The cycle continued.

A new job opportunity came along, and Payton decided he wanted to start it sober. He tried abstinence cold turkey but the physical sickness of withdrawal always drew him back to taking another pill. He called an opioid quitline and the representative told him he needed in-patient addiction treatment. Payton knew if he took that much time off work he would lose his role as executive chef and start at the bottom when he returned. He hung up, feeling the familiar weight of rejection. "It felt like he was telling me the only way I could get better was on his terms. On the terms of these rehabs. And I knew that wasn't true," Payton remembers.

He felt he was making conscious decisions to buy every pill he took, so he decided to make a new conscious decision. He would wean himself off of opioids while filling his life up with meaningful activities and relationships to take their place. Lining up his pills for the week, he budgeted them for each day, trying to use a little less over time. Sometimes the withdrawal symptoms were bad enough that he took an extra half a pill just to take the edge off the sickness, but over time he got down to just one in the morning and half a pill in the afternoon. Emptying his life of pills was only half the strategy, though. He focused just as much on filling it up with hobbies, exercise, and healthy relationships. He understood that stopping the pills without filling the void was unlikely to last.

One afternoon at two o'clock he went to the bathroom at work to take half a pill. He looked at his watch, thinking about all the food orders he'd prepared for lunch and all the coming ones for dinner. Then he stared at the white half pill in his other hand and made the decision. "I cannot take this," he said to himself and put it back in his pocket. He had taken his last recreational pill. He still has that last half a pill several years later, kept as a symbol of the end of that season in his life.

A few years after that afternoon in the bathroom at work, he had an abscessed tooth and the doctor gave him pain pills. He took them as directed and felt the familiar buzzed feeling kick in. For some people, taking pain pills for medical reasons after beating an addiction triggers a relapse. For others, like Payton, it reminded him of the life he didn't want to lead anymore. "I recognized the feeling, but I didn't need it because there was already enough joy in my life. Before, that feeling was filling a void, whereas now there weren't many voids."

Today Payton is sober, married, and serves as the executive chef of a popular restaurant a few minutes from my house. His climb out of addiction isn't the story we hear most. It lacks the clean lines of addiction > treatment > total abstinence. Payton never hit "rock bottom," never went to treatment, and hasn't been totally abstinent. Yet he was addicted to opioids for years and today is not. He didn't take the quantum leap. He built his own staircase, taking one step at a time toward a fulfilling life, leaving the void and the drugs that filled it behind.

RELAPSE

Each individual's steps toward a thriving life will look different. Each one might take an excruciatingly long time. A person might remain on that first step of "staying alive" for years. But as long as they're alive, there's hope. One day they might be ready to take another step, but it can only happen if the flame of life is not snuffed out first.

Even when someone takes a few more steps, they probably won't be in the order we think they should be. Backward motion is as likely as forward motion too. When relapse happens, what do we do? Revert to holding the hammer over their heads?

My friend Thom is in recovery today, but only after many relapses on his journey out of addiction. It's easy to understand the draw of drugs when you hear him talk about what they did for him. "The world had a rosy glow about it," he describes. "It was just like everything was in its proper place." Sounds like a very compelling experience to me, when so much of the world is hard and broken and out of order. It was for Thom, so he has a tender place in his heart for relapse and what a person needs when they're in the middle of it. "When someone relapses," says Thom with conviction, "what they need more than anything else is they need even more love and even more support and even more people around them. They don't need shame. They don't need somebody beating them up about it, because they're doing all of that 10 times more than anybody else ever could.

They need love." Celebrating one step at a time, and offering encouragement and support even when those steps are in the wrong direction, might be the best way to help more people make it out of the darkness and into the light.

It should be noted that backward motion is just as likely with the quantum leap approach as it is with the stair-step approach. There are no silver bullets to be found anywhere. Just different pathways that may work better for some people. A living person on the first step is far better than a dead person who tried for the top too soon. Thriving lives are only possible with living people. There are thousands of grieving families who have found out through unspeakable loss that a quantum leap to abstinence was too much, too fast. There are a few people who stick that landing permanently, but with a street drug supply that's so toxic and the risk of relapse so high, it might be worth considering stair steps. It won't produce a person's best life overnight, but it could save their life.

Most of us have been taught that people can't have a meaningful life until they beat their addiction, but I wonder if that's backward. Maybe people can't beat addiction until they have a meaningful life.

That doesn't mean there's no accountability or consequences. There are many other ways to hold people accountable than arresting them. A wife might tell her husband that unless he addresses his addiction he has to move out. Or a parent might tell their addicted child that because they stole money from mom's wallet, they can't spend the night at home anymore. If an addicted person steals your lawn mower and pawns it in order to get money to fund their addiction, they'll still be arrested for theft. All of us face consequences for our actions, and good boundaries are crucial with addiction. But we can set up good boundaries while encouraging our loved ones to take one step toward a healthier life. We can celebrate each step of progress instead of withholding our approval until they've checked every box. We can let them know that our love for them isn't contingent on whether or not they use drugs. We can share our dream of a fulfilling life for them. Maybe even help them rekindle that dream in themselves.

A HAND TO HOLD

Right now we're in a pressure cooker of extremes. The battle for control and coercion rages between addicted people, their families, police, and treatment centers. It all hinges on the idea that we can force recovery. That we can make people choose what we think is best for them. That it can happen on our timeline, often overnight. That we can control someone else. Millions of families can attest to the infuriating reality that we can't control people or their addictions, even though we cry, scream, beg, threaten, lock up, bail out, cut off, or enable. We don't have control of hurting people. What if we let go of the imaginary grip we wish we had, and offered a hand to hold instead?

Christi Berrong-Barber was told to cut her son off, to let him crash and hit rock bottom on his own, but she couldn't do that. She wanted to be certain that if the call came that Chance was dead, she would have no regrets. "Chance is my son and I'll never give up," she says. The only way she could live without regrets was to pursue a healthy relationship with her son when it was possible, even through the chaos of his unhealthy choices. Christi's dream of the day Chance decides to pursue recovery for himself hasn't been realized yet. This is the situation millions of families are in. Their loved one has a problematic relationship with substances but isn't ready or able to make a change. What do they do? More and more families are finding and implementing the research-based Community Reinforcement and Family Training (CRAFT) method. It was developed specifically for loved ones of people struggling with addiction who aren't interested in making a change yet. It teaches people how to take care of themselves while also engaging in constructive ways with their loved one, using communication and support methods that have been proven to increase the likelihood the person struggling will make a real change for the better. The options aren't "cut them off" or "let them walk all over you." CRAFT teaches families how to stay connected and have the best chance of influencing their loved one without getting drawn into the chaos.

Christi's commitment to celebrating small steps and being part of that journey to healing for Chance has extended to many other people too. Recently she started the Molly Angel Project. Named after Chance's girlfriend who died of an overdose, Molly Angel gives the opioid overdose reversal medication naloxone to anyone who needs it. Many times that means Christi is venturing into parts of town most people avoid and connecting with people whose addictions have taken everything from them. Her background in the medical field often comes in handy as she teaches people about wound care, a constant problem when dirty needles and contaminated drugs are all many people have access to. These are the people Christi believes God has called her to love and care for.

She's not trying to change the world. She's trying to help one son or daughter at a time stay alive and take small steps forward, so they have the chance to find healing. And when their lives end in heartbreak, she's there for that too.

In the last 12 months Christi has attended 7 funerals for people who haven't even reached their 21st birthday. She has determined that she'll be a stepping stone toward connection and healing for the families too. "The mothers are always surprised to see me there. Because after a while you feel like your kids..." Christi pauses and continues through tears, "You see your baby. You see your child. You see the little person that you raised, but you realize that nobody else sees them anymore." Christi pauses again. "That's the thing that hurts the most sometimes. Even though I remember my son, nobody else sees him for who he is once he's an addict or an inmate. He's a number. He's a thing. But he's still the little boy that took all the doorknobs off my doors because he wanted to know how they worked."

The idea of stair steps pushes against the idea that people have to hit "rock bottom" and then make the quantum leap in order to enter recovery, and it also pushes against the idea that people need to have a moment of spiritual awakening to enter recovery. Questioning the deeply interwoven fabric of recovery and faith in the South seems like touching the Holy Grail, but I think we may actually be damaging people's spiritual wellbeing as well as their health by forging a marriage between two things that can go together but don't have to.

CHAPTER 22

INGREDIENTS FOR TRANSFORMATION

The last office on the right is Branden Henry's. I've been in several therapists' offices over the years as I've navigated the pain of life in a world gone wrong, but never his. Scanning the room as I walk in, I notice it's very personalized to him. A guitar sits off to one side of the sofa, and the cozy space is decorated with art and mementos that show his love of the outdoors. Several times a year he takes groups of men on outdoor adventure trips built around healing and community. The light brown leather sofa creaks as I sink into it, and Branden settles into his chair across from me. I'm here to chat as a friend, not for therapy, but by the time I leave I'll feel the familiar sense of clarity that I so often experience in that setting.

On my learning journey I've had several really helpful conversations with Branden because he specializes in helping people who are struggling with addictions, and today I stopped by to ask him about the complexities of faith, addiction, and recovery. All three are close to his heart because he's a Christian in recovery himself.

Branden grew up in a straight-laced Christian home in Arkansas and experienced a lot of trauma throughout his childhood. He first used food to numb the pain, and when he found pornography and later alcohol, his addictions multiplied. His theory was that if his addictions were bad, his good works had to be better. So after he got married, he taught school in the Mississippi Delta, led a youth ministry and went to seminary to become a therapist. But healing doesn't work that way. "You just can't perform your way out of pain," Branden told me with a sad smile in one of our earlier conversations.

When he and his wife and four kids moved to Mississippi so he could go to graduate school, they came to our church. I had no idea the father and husband sitting a few pews ahead of me in church week after week was struggling with multiple addictions. Everything looked ok on the outside, as it so often does with us church folk. We tend to be very good at putting on masks. But inside he was dying.

He stumbled on a men's group in Jackson that offered unconditional love and acceptance. No performance needed. Even though he was in school to learn how to help other people heal, he began to experience healing for himself in their company. It led him to a therapist who helped him begin to heal the root causes of his own addictions. But even with a supportive community and therapy, it was two more years before he was able to stop drinking. Healing takes time. Now Branden has spent the last decade as a therapist, helping other people on their own healing journeys.

As I shift in my seat, the sun filtering through the window lights up the writing on the glass markerboard above Branden's desk, I ask his thoughts on how he approaches addiction and recovery through the lens of his faith as well as the lens of his training in trauma. I'm curious how churches can help people who are struggling, now that we know so much more about the root causes of addiction. Branden shares his observations from the Bible on how Jesus responds to hurting people whose lives are visibly broken. In Scripture, Jesus tends to follow a pattern of looking for humility, extending mercy, and then calling to action, Branden explains. When he meets someone who has already been humbled, like the woman caught in adultery in John chapter eight, he extends mercy and then calls her to a changed life. When he engages with people who haven't yet been humbled, he calls them first to humility, like the rich man in Mark chapter ten. When they embrace humility and recognize their need, he extends mercy. A changed life follows.

I've never thought about this before, and it strikes me because it's the opposite of our approach to many people struggling with all manner of brokenness. We want action first, offering mercy only when we see a changed life. We don't want them to think their bad behavior is no big deal, so we save our mercy until we're satisfied that change has happened.

But Jesus does not relate to people this way. He doesn't withhold his love and mercy until He's satisfied that enough action has been taken. Jesus calls us to come to Him with our nothing and receive His everything. Only then do we begin the process of change and transformation by the Holy Spirit living in us. The good news of the Gospel - the thing that makes Christianity different from every other major religion - is that God doesn't meet us with a yardstick to measure our performance. He doesn't sit on His throne and wait for us to work our way to His feet. *He* comes to *us*, meeting us at our lowest points with a cascading waterfall of love, grace, and mercy. I'm staking my eternal life on the spiritual truth that mercy precedes transformation, not the other way around.

After working with addicted people for years, Branden is also convinced that this Gospel lesson applies to addiction. We often want changed behavior before we're willing to offer connection, love, belonging, and purpose. As uncomfortable and complicated as it is, people often need those first.

This is a hard tension, one Branden is the first to admit. Every day in his practice he sees the onslaught of destruction that addiction can cause in families. It can destroy the relationships and connections that provide the very things needed for healing. And yet, those needs are still there, often deeper than ever.

Maybe this is where the broader community and the faith community can play a key role. Could we lay down our own yardsticks for performance and be a stepping-stone on the journey to recovery for people whose closest relationships are strained to the point of breaking? Joanne's life was changed through the power of many people being stepping-stones. The NICU nurses who treated her with kindness and the social worker who valued her role as a mother were early ones, giving her family relationships time to heal. Sometimes the broader community is better positioned than family to provide stepping-stones, especially during those first steps. We don't have to be the whole path, just one stepping-stone.

NOT REQUIRED

Along those lines, one of the things we in the faith community may need to expand our understanding of is the relationship between faith and recovery. A lot of people, especially here in the South, believe addiction can only be overcome through a personal relationship with Jesus.

Addiction certainly can have deep spiritual components, and I believe everyone needs Jesus whether or not they're addicted, but following Jesus doesn't make the brokenness of the world or the wounds we carry disappear. Struggles and wounds of many kinds linger, often until heaven. A Christian who still struggles with addiction is no less of a Christian than one who doesn't. They're on a journey of transformation like every other child of God.

Telling addicted people that the only way they can overcome a complex health crisis is by embracing a particular approach to faith creates a two-fold problem. First, it's simply not true. Many people move past addictions every day without becoming Christians or even believing in a higher power. Second, people can become Christians and still struggle with addiction.

Recovery isn't a transaction with God where I put my faith in him and he stops my addiction. There are some people who have a Damascus road experience of spiritual transformation and they find their addiction suddenly in the rearview mirror. That's incredible! But for most people, Christians and non-Christians alike, the journey out of addiction is a lot slower, with fits and starts and failures and successes. Faith can be a powerful part of someone's recovery journey, but it isn't required, and it's no guarantee. Coercing people to follow Jesus by holding their recovery hostage to conversion is not biblical and can destroy people spiritually when their allegiance doesn't solve their addiction. Such a view can derail healthy recovery *and* healthy faith.

In the same way that law enforcement officers tend to have significant aversion to rethinking our drug laws, there can be similar aversion in the faith and treatment communities to rethinking the centrality of a spiritual conversion in addiction recovery. Many people and many programs have fused faith and recovery tightly together, but if we want to help more people find a path out of addiction, acknowledging that recovery is possible no matter what people believe seems very important. For people who want a faith-based experience, those programs can be incredibly helpful. But no path out of addiction should be stigmatized, and as with other health crises, we should listen to the research on effective treatments. All of us are susceptible to confirmation bias when a new idea encroaches on an existing one, but if we want to help more people find a path to recovery that works for them, we need to stay curious.

Approaching recovery as a step-by-step journey toward a thriving life instead of a quantum leap to the goal reminds me a little of my own faith journey. Even though I've been a Christian for 30 years, I'm continually frustrated at how agonizingly slow my spiritual growth has been. Seasons of daily Scripture reading are followed by droughts of my Bible gathering dust on the shelf. Times of growth are followed by long stretches of apathy. The process of being made more like Jesus feels a lot like the imperceptible growth of an oak tree. I can only see it when I measure year to year or decade to decade, not day to day. Most change in life is slow like that. If Jesus can walk with me one step at a time on the winding road to spiritual growth, I think it honors His image in another person to offer them one step at a time on the winding road out of the darkness and into the light.

Shifting to a step-by-step approach to recovery is no easy path. There are none of those where addiction is present. But what's the alternative? Put more people in the pressure cooker and turn up the heat? If that worked well, addiction would've been solved decades ago. Maybe we can try something different. If we did, it would also open the door for more people to access the most effective form of treatment for opioid addiction available right now.

CHAPTER 23

SOBER ANOTHER WAY

Staring up, my eyes follow the ceiling fan as it slowly spins, reminding me that it's been quite a while since I dusted it. When I wait too long, the dust starts falling in little clumps onto the bedspread where I'm laying now. That's life with little kids, though. The list is endless, and dusting ceiling fans falls at the bottom of the priority list. It's "rest time" for the boys and I'm taking the opportunity of peace and quiet to listen as Michele tells me her story over the phone. I met her along this learning journey, and today she's sharing how she finally found recovery after years of opioid addiction and several overdoses.

Michele grew up in a sheltered Christian home a couple of hours south of Jackson, MS. Drugs weren't part of her childhood, but trauma was. She witnessed a murder when she was just 11 years old, but she had been taught to be tough, work hard, and move forward. So she did, locking the pain away and becoming a successful cosmetologist as an adult.

After 20 years as a hairstylist, a burning sensation in her hip wouldn't go away. She was diagnosed with congenital hip dysplasia that required surgery, but her doctor recommended she wait as long as she could for it. Without health insurance, putting off the surgery made sense financially too. The hip pain was severe, and a friend gave her a few opioid pills that really helped.

The pills helped so much that she found a doctor to prescribe them, and I can't help but think of Dr. Alexander and Rat Park as Michele told me what those pills did for her. "When I took opiates, it didn't just numb the physical pain, it numbed the emotional pain too," she explained. The internal pain she'd spent years trying to outrun was suddenly muted. What a powerful experience. As her opioid tolerance increased, as it naturally does, her doctor increased her dose. Even then, she began taking more pills than she was supposed to, then more pills than her doctor would prescribe. Her life began to slowly spin out of control as her focus became getting pills anywhere she could. Her relationships with her mother, daughter, and friends started to crumble.

Although she survived two overdoses herself, she wasn't able to save her fiancé, who died of a fentanyl overdose. "My parents tried tough love with me, but it didn't work," Michele remembers. She already felt ashamed. Already blamed herself. More of the same didn't help. "Did I loathe myself in addiction?

Loathe isn't a strong enough word. I felt like a dog," Michele said emphatically when I asked her how she felt about herself during these years. "I knew I wasn't that person, but I was doing these things that I hated so much. I hated myself."

Over the years, Michele tried to stop using drugs many times, without success. The sickness of withdrawal always sent her back. She was desperate for another path. "I knew there was help out there, and I started searching," Michele told me in a determined voice. She found a doctor who prescribed the medication buprenorphine. It, along with medication such as methadone and naltrexone, is used to treat various drug addictions through what's known as Medication-Assisted Treatment (MAT) or Medications for Opioid Use Disorder (MOUD).

Accompanying her to the doctor, Michele's dad also heard an explanation of what had happened to his daughter over the last 11 years as the opioids that once helped her had destroyed her life. Before this, her family just thought she'd gone crazy. The doctor started Michele on buprenorphine that day, and over the next several years Michele got up in the morning, put the paper-thin strip of medication under her tongue where it dissolved, and went about rebuilding her relationships, career, and health.

"My life is one thousand times better than it was when I was addicted. It's been the best time of my life other than my daughter being born," says Michele with a smile. The rebuilding hasn't been a straight shot to glory, though. Addiction causes deep pain for the people who love the addicted person. That trauma lingers too. "It takes so much time to gain trust back. My dad has been my rock. People really do need a support system in recovery. I've restored my relationships with my family – my mom, my dad, my daughter. They trust me now," Michele says.

"People need to know that there is a life after addiction," she continues with passion. "Some people need to have MAT. They just do. Forcing people to do it through abstinence can kill you." That may seem like an exaggerated statement, but it's exactly what happened to the son of my friend Jessie Dunleavy.

Jessie's son, struggling with opioid addiction, asked her to please help him find a way to access MAT. While Jessie searched for a doctor who would prescribe it, one of them raised his voice at her and said her son didn't need MAT. It wouldn't solve his addiction and he might be on it for the rest of his life, the doctor fumed. As Jessie continued searching, her son bought drugs off the street and died from an overdose. "Buprenorphine is an FDA-approved medication with a long track record of helping people get over their addiction, and it's hard to get," Jessie tells me with exasperation in her voice. "But street drugs are easy to get," she points out. Jessie wishes she could go back to the conversation with that doctor and tell him what she knows now: At least her son would still be alive. As long as there's life, there's opportunity. "MAT doesn't prolong addiction," she says. "It prolongs life."

It's baffling to me why MAT is sometimes stigmatized or scoffed at. For opioid addiction, it has the least risk of death and the highest rates of long-term sobriety of any treatment currently available.[8] It's possible to misuse these medications too, but they're still considered the gold standard in opioid addiction treatment today. I can't imagine someone scoffing at the most effective cancer treatment or the most effective smoking cessation aid. For no other medical condition do we encourage people to skip the most effective forms of treatment and try less effective ones first.

MAT has the added benefit of not only reducing harm to the person struggling with addiction but reducing harm to the community too. A stabilized, successfully treated person no longer needs to engage in crime to support their habit. They can work and pay taxes, are less likely to end up in the emergency room, they're able to take care of their children again, and so on. Everyone wins when MAT is successful.

No treatment works for everyone, but for many people, MAT removes their cravings and allows them to stabilize their life and begin building a better one. MAT isn't something I knew much about until after I'd changed my mind about the big picture of drug policy. But even in a world where drugs are handled as a health issue from production to consumption, some people will still use them, and we need to have the best tools at hand to prevent addiction and treat it when it develops. Research clearly shows that MAT is one of those tools.

For Michele, buprenorphine allowed her to build a thriving life again and simply feel normal. "I get up in the morning and take my medication," she told me. "I have no other feelings other than being normal. I don't understand the stigma behind it." When I asked Michele how she would describe her addiction and then her time in recovery on MAT, this is the picture she painted: "The best way I can describe it is imagine the darkest, darkest night with no stars, no hope, no light whatsoever and you're lost. And then you think about the most beautiful day and surroundings you ever hope to see. That's the difference between my addiction and my recovery. It feels like two different lives. I had lost all hope of restoration with my family. I had lost all hope of ever being out of the rat race of chasing-chasing-chasing pills. I thought I would die without those pills. I couldn't imagine any kind of future. I could never imagine my life now. I've had a second chance at life, and I'm taking it. I'm so happy. I don't even have words for how I feel now. To wake up and feel like a normal person now, it's worth everything," she says with hope, lifting her voice. "It's not trading one addiction for another. I have a normal life now. I have a great life now. I didn't have that before."

Michele's experience reminded me of a conversation I had with an addiction doctor about MAT. I told him about the woman who called me after my newspaper article and shared about her daughter's heroin addiction and all the money their family had spent on the best treatment centers, to no avail. The one thing she was adamant about was that her daughter not attend a center that offered MAT. She considered that to be "trading one addiction for another." As I asked the doctor what he thought about that conversation, he told me sadly, "They may have sent their daughter to the most expensive treatment centers, but they weren't the best in terms of outcomes unless they offered Medication Assisted Treatment."

In my experience, people who found sobriety through abstinence can have a lot of investment aversion to MAT. Our culture has had a singular focus on abstinence as the bar for success for a long time, and the commitment to it runs very deep. It seems to me that effective treatments shouldn't be controversial, though, even if they don't work for everyone and not everyone chooses them.

Some people use medications like methadone or buprenorphine for a time and eventually taper off. For others, it's permanent. They may build a thriving life while on MAT and decide with their doctor that staying on it is what's best for them. There are many health challenges people face that require long-term medication. Sometimes it feels like we value an abstinent dead person more than a living person using medication. I don't think we mean to do this, but our focus on total abstinence even when it risks someone's life and health is concerning to me. If my own child was struggling with an opioid addiction, wouldn't I encourage them to try the most effective treatment first? If that didn't work, then branching out into other options would make sense.

Allowing people struggling with addiction to access MAT without barriers or stigma would make it much easier to stay alive and build a thriving life. Jessie Dunleavy is right that street drugs are available to anyone, anywhere, with no barriers. It shouldn't be easier to get heroin than it is to get buprenorphine. Some states need policy change to remove barriers to MAT, but just about every community needs a heart change to break down misplaced stigmas and open the door to as many options for recovery as there are people who can be helped by them.

CHAPTER 24

TWO THRIVING LIVES

Avideo starts playing as I scroll through Facebook. A man is onstage playing a guitar at what looks like a local music festival. I glance at whose post this is, and it's Joanne's. I look closer and behind the man, almost hidden by a full set of black and silver drums, is a child. Is that really Beckham? Yes it is. Joanne has been posting videos of Beckham dancing in front of the stage at festivals like this since he was a toddler, but now he's *on* the stage and *playing* in the festival as an accomplished little drummer at just seven years old. It fills my heart with joy to see Beckham where he should be - with his mom as she records all

30 minutes of his playing time and posts it to Facebook and as she makes t-shirts for all the extended family that say "I'm with the drummer." I get to enjoy their success from afar, but Joanne is the one who has done all the hard work to live in recovery and build this life for them day by day.

(Joanne and Beckham today)

She and I have stayed in touch since that day when I dropped Beckham back off with her when she was still in treatment. They live a couple of hours away so we don't see each other often, but we've had several opportunities to reflect on how the path we walked together changed both of us. I've asked Joanne many questions about her experience of addiction and what it has been like to live in recovery.

She describes her many years of addiction this way: "Emptiness. Hopeless. Despair. Lonely. Anxious. Sad. A very, very dark place." But if you meet Joanne, you won't find someone focused on what was lost in those years. You'll find a woman full of the joy of the Lord, quick to remind you how good God is and how thankful she is for every step He's helped her take. Many of those steps are things most people take for granted. Today, she can be on time for an appointment instead of 2 hours late. She wakes up, eats breakfast, and has coffee. A morning routine was foreign during addiction. She laughs as she tells me what else she loves about sobriety. "I'm probably one of the happiest people on the first of the month when I can pay my bills. I'm grateful for that." She's able to support herself and her son, which she describes as an honor. She has insurance on her car now, and when the starter went out on it a couple of weeks ago, she had the money to buy the part and fix it. Just like that. In active addiction, the car would've sat for months while she tried to save up the money. Today she fills her tank all the way up when she gets gas. "I was never able to put a full tank of gas in my car because I never had $20 at one time," she says, reflecting on life before sobriety. She always managed enough money to buy cigarettes or other drugs, but everything else was just survival day to day.

One of her biggest accomplishments of sobriety is the first vacation she took with just her and Beckham. They went to

Gatlinburg, TN, and enjoyed all the sights, experiences, and tastes that so many other families enjoy without realizing what a gift it is. That kind of trip is something she never would've thought was possible during her years of active addiction or even early in her recovery. Saving money for a trip. Planning a trip. Being sober for that many days in a row. For most of her adult life, the days revolved around getting enough drugs just to function. Now she's free from her life orbiting around drugs. Today it orbits around her relationship with God, service at her church, raising her son, and working full-time. She's also about to open a sober living home for a mother with children. She describes these years of sobriety this way: "Joy, happiness, wholeness, love, compassion, and empathy." Such a stark contrast to the darkness before.

One evening as Joanne and I talked about her journey to recovery, I asked her why she couldn't exit addiction until after Beckham was born. I knew she'd wanted to be a mom her whole life, and when she unexpectedly got pregnant after years of doctors telling her she would never have a child, she was overjoyed. Why wasn't it pregnancy that triggered the transformation? She doesn't know. She's just as baffled as most people are by the path of their addiction. Addiction is so complex, our lives are so complex, and it's not easy to pinpoint when or why a change happens. But she's sure of one thing. Even the smallest act of kindness or a gentle word can greatly affect someone's recovery. She can still name all the nurses who took care of Beckham in the NICU after he was born. She often reminds me that on our first phone call, I asked her if she wanted Beckham to have a pacifier. That simple question made her feel valuable and important as his mother. It gave her a voice.

Today the tiny baby that fused my life to Joanne's is a handsome boy who loves to play at parks and makes a friend everywhere he goes. For a treat, he loves to eat sushi with his mom.

Even with the most health-centered, evidence-based, non-punitive approach to addiction, we don't always get outcomes like Joanne and Beckham. Nothing is guaranteed. But if she was sitting in prison, there definitely would be no sushi dates, no playgrounds, and no trips together.

FOR THE BABIES, FOR THE MOMS

Celebrating Joanne's success doesn't diminish the seriousness of her choices while she was pregnant. Prenatal drug use is not healthy and can cause harm to children. It's so tempting to grab the stick instead of the carrot and punish moms whose choices put their children at risk. Some states have adopted a practice of charging pregnant women criminally if they expose their unborn children to drugs. It's often touted as a way to protect babies. As well-intended as these laws may be, we have to step back and ask this key question: What is the best way to protect the lives of unborn children whose mothers are struggling with addiction? Prosecution or prenatal care? If a woman is afraid that a doctor's visit will land her in prison, that momma won't go anywhere near a doctor for as long as possible. It seems to me that the impact these prosecutions are most likely to have on unborn children is to incentivize women struggling with addiction to have an abortion. If they give their child life, they could spend the next decade in prison. If they have an abortion, they won't.

If we want addicted moms like Joanne to make healthier choices early in their pregnancies, we have to broaden the path to help, not scare them away from it. Again, intent doesn't equal outcome.

THE KEY

I want to make it abundantly clear that what *happened to* me is different than what *changed in* me, because it's key to avoiding more policy failures. Joanne didn't change my mind about our drug laws. She changed my *heart* about people who use drugs, which got me curious to start learning. It was the evidence and research I was exposed to on that learning journey that changed my *mind* about the best laws to reduce harm.

We get into deep trouble by taking our personal experiences and projecting them onto everyone. Just because someone had shoulder surgery and became addicted to opioids doesn't mean everyone who has shoulder surgery does. Just because someone used marijuana and had a terrible mental health reaction doesn't mean everyone who uses marijuana does. When we hold up a personal experience as a universal experience, and then make laws based on it, very bad things can happen. Drug-induced homicide laws are an example of this.

Loved ones of people who have died of overdose rightly want to do something to help the problem. Unfortunately, some of them have taken a page out of the last 100 years of punitive drug policy and asked for dealers to be prosecuted for murder when someone dies from an overdose. Research on the topic fails to show that these laws reduce overdose deaths, but they do create a lot of additional harm. People sell drugs to friends or share drugs at parties all the time. As a result, these laws are often used against a close friend or family member, not some big-time drug dealer. They also incentivize people to flee the scene instead of staying and helping someone suffering from an overdose. Do we really want to make it scarier for someone to stick around and call for help, risking whatever concoction of charges the prosecution might be able to lay on them? We're talking about human beings here. Scared, probably inebriated human beings at that. Our policies need to be built for the real world, based on research and evidence, not emotion and personal experience. That includes my own emotions and personal experiences. Laws apply to *everyone*.

There is one caveat to that last principle that's important to highlight. Laws do apply to everyone, but they're not always enforced against everyone equally. African Americans are far more likely to be arrested on a drug charge than white people are. If they were committing drug crimes at higher rates, that would make sense, but they're not. They're just arrested for them far more frequently.

Disproportionate enforcement has meant that, tragically, minority communities have experienced significantly more damage from punitive drug policies. The generational impact from this concentration of harm is hard to overstate. Racial bias is also deeply woven into the history of how drug prohibition began.

All of this is worthy of deep lament.

For some people, their case for ending prohibition rests on the reality of disproportionate enforcement. I respect their perspective and passion for justice, but if disproportionate enforcement was the core problem with prohibition, other people could make the case that we simply need *more* cops and *more* arrests to even out the disparity. Other groups are committing the same crimes, after all. They're just not getting arrested as often. This is not the answer.

The racial aspect of punitive drug policies has been well-researched and written about in many other books. I've chosen not to spend very much time on it here because this book is about my experiences and the journey of changing my mind. I happen to be white, Joanne is white, and most of the stories in this book are about people who are white, including the courtroom experience with the pregnant woman pleading for her fiancé's freedom. My experiences didn't expose me to the racially disproportionate aspects of enforcement until later in my journey.

What changed my mind about the best path forward with drugs was learning about the human cost of prohibition. That harm is present regardless of a person's race, income, or ethnicity. Racially disproportionate enforcement is an additional layer of devastating harm, but even if there was no racial bias in the past or present, the practical outcomes of prohibition remain. A criminal justice approach to drugs and drug use is harmful *even when it is proportionately enforced*. Arresting more white people or fewer black people wouldn't fix the core problems with drug policy. Those have to be fixed at the policy level, not the enforcement level.

So what did I do with everything I experienced and learned after meeting Joanne? Told other people, of course! The problem was, I was pretty terrified of what other people might think. If they knew I now supported ending drug prohibition and implementing some form of legal access for adults, would they think I'd lost my mind? My faith? My values? Would they listen long enough to understand why?

I decided to find out.

CHAPTER 25

END IT FOR GOOD

Agonizing over what to say and how to say it, I finally decide my commentary is ready. My fingers take a break from typing and run along the scratched edge of my yard sale desk that doubles as the nightstand on my side of the bed. Our house has such an open floor plan that our bedroom is the only place where I can be guaranteed some quiet…at least until a fight breaks out among the boys or someone needs help with their schoolwork. I stare out the window at my neighbor's banana tree. The fact that a banana tree can grow in Mississippi lets you know something about the climate of our summers, but it's all I've ever known. I've never lived anywhere but Mississippi.

My eyes return to the screen in front of me where I've been typing the longest Facebook post in my social media history. I know long posts are a drag for people to read, but I'm so nervous that I'll be misunderstood that paragraph after paragraph of explanation pours out of my fingers. It's April, 2017, and my hands are visibly shaking from nerves as I take a deep breath and hit the post button. It's the first time I've publicly shared my change of mind in favor of a health-centered approach to drugs instead of a criminal justice one. It's been 18 months since I met Joanne and I'm still very new to the approach I now support.

Immediately a vulnerability hangover sets in. What have I done? What will people think? I've built a reputation as a dependable, trustworthy woman who is committed to the Lord and who gets things done, especially at church. Will people look at me differently? Will their trust erode? Will they have the same reaction to me that I did to the people of California when I heard they had legalized marijuana? It's hard to overstate how scary it is to step outside the tribe. Will their curiosity be sparked like mine was, or will they think I've just gone off the deep end?

Getting up to get the kids a snack, I come back to check on the post frequently. Even though only a few people engage as the day passes, it gets me over the hump of sharing my perspective publicly for the first time. Nothing explodes, no one yells at me, and a few people even seem intrigued.

Over the next 2 months, I get a little braver, posting a few more times. In July I decide to host a book discussion of the book I found most helpful on my learning journey, Johann Hari's *Chasing the Scream*. On July 28, the day after my 34th birthday, 12 people gather in a meeting room at Corner Bakery, books in hand, and discuss the ideas in Johann's book. A lot of the people don't know each other. The common thread is they're either related to me or they commented on one of my hesitant Facebook posts. My middle brother, Joel, is a State Representative now in the Mississippi Legislature, so I invite him to come and answer questions about Mississippi drug policy and how laws are made and changed.

The group ranges in age from a recent college grad to a set of grandparents. There's a former prosecutor and a social worker, an attorney, and a stay-at-home mom. It's a diverse group, and here we are in Jackson, Mississippi, discussing the idea of making more drugs legal for adult use as a possible way to reduce harm overall. What kind of twilight zone is this? We talk until the restaurant closes, then stand on the sidewalk and talk longer. The energy of the evening feels like momentum. As I walk to my minivan in the dark, I look back at a couple of people who are still chatting and have a very clear thought: "This could be something."

I hosted another discussion dinner with a new group of people 6 months later, more than doubling the attendance of the first one. Over the next year, I hosted 3 more. By this point almost 150 people had read *Chasing the Scream* and attended one of these discussions in Mississippi. Most of them weren't people I knew before they attended the discussion. They'd heard about it from a friend or coworker. When I met James Moore through that email exchange in April 2018 after I wrote an article in the newspaper, he didn't know I was hosting these book discussions. I invited him to come to Jackson for one of them, but instead, he invited me to come to Hattiesburg and lead one. "But James," I said, "I don't know anyone in Hattiesburg except you. Who's going to come?" Word of mouth was the only way people found out about the discussions at this point. James assured me that if

I came and led the discussion, he would fill the room. And he did. Thirty people crammed into a small meeting room at Chesterfield's restaurant in Hattiesburg. "This could be something" passed through my mind again.

It's hard to articulate the experience of being in a room full of people from such diverse backgrounds, many of them Christians and conservatives like me, all having an honest and civil dialogue about the merits of ending drug prohibition and shifting to a health-centered approach to drugs and addiction. At one discussion, several judges came and one of them leaned over to the attorney sitting next to him, who happened to be a friend of mine, and said, "I can't believe this is happening in Jackson, Mississippi." We're one of the most conservative and religious states in the country and these events were drawing law enforcement officers, elected officials, business owners, doctors, attorneys, parents whose children were struggling with addiction, and people in early recovery. It was a twilight zone in the best of ways! Not only were people truly interested in learning, they were hungry for real solutions, even if those solutions challenged the status quo. Some people were most interested in how to stop overdose. Others were most intrigued by the potential to significantly reduce violent crime. Others didn't want their tax dollars wasted and were curious if ending the arrest of people for drug possession might be a big step toward fiscal responsibility. Others had loved ones who couldn't provide for their families because they had a felony.

"Are you going to do another one of these? I know some people who would be interested in coming," was something I heard after every discussion. Hosting them and facilitating respectful dialogue was so life-giving to me, and it was also a great way to keep learning. I kept notes on people's comments and questions during the discussion time at each event, then went home and built my knowledge by finding the answers. I wanted this tiny movement toward life and health to grow!

ACCELERATION

Just a few weeks after the first book discussion in Hattiesburg, a former narcotics officer named Juan Cloy heard about the discussion events and invited me to give a presentation to a group of community leaders in Jackson. The kicker, though, was they weren't going to read *Chasing the Scream* beforehand like the events I'd led so far. I would have to make the case for my new perspective on drugs and addiction from scratch. Not wanting to turn down an opportunity to invite more people into the conversation, I pulled up a generic slide presentation template and filled it in with my best effort at putting what I'd learned into my own words, with some free clipart for visuals. The finishing touches got finalized with my laptop propped against the steering wheel as I sat in my van in the parking lot of the coffee shop where the group was meeting, collecting my thoughts before I went in.

Jonathan Lee, one of the men who was there that morning, thought the presentation was compelling. Unbeknownst to me he told his friend Pam Shaw, who was on the TEDx Jackson conference committee, about it. A few days later I got an email with an invitation to apply as a speaker for the TEDx event that was just six weeks away. What?! Giving a TEDx Talk would be a dream come true!

The train wreck when I was 15 exposed me to a lot of new experiences, including throwing me into the deep end of public speaking. The morning after the wreck, my phone at the hotel started ringing. Reporters were calling to ask if they could interview me about my experience. My name was the first one released publicly on the survivors list, and we were the only Bomgaars family in Mississippi so it was easy for reporters to find my parents and then me.

Over the next two days, before we flew home to Jackson, I gave numerous live interviews on national television, even appearing on The Today Show. It gave me a vision for the way sharing my perspective could help other people understand something better, but also for the importance of respecting people's stories. When I called Mom and Dad to tell them I was going to be interviewed on tv, Mom said, "Christina, don't ever forget that even though being on tv is a new experience for you and probably exciting, there are families who just lost a loved one in the same accident you're sharing about. Remember them." Those interviews showed me the power of communication up close, as well as the responsibility. A few weeks after the wreck I was able to share in front of my church and then for the chapel service at the Air National Guard base in Jackson, where Dad was the chaplain's assistant. As I stood in front of several hundred soldiers sharing about the wreck and the goodness of God, I lost all track of time and accidentally became the longest-speaking chapel guest in Dad's career, as he vainly tried to catch my attention and signal to wrap up.

To me, giving a TEDx Talk would be the ultimate opportunity to take what I learned at a young age about the power of communication and translate what I learned about drugs and addiction into a message that could help more people see it through a different lens. At the same time, I wanted desperately to honor the stories and experiences of people who have paid the ultimate price for our failed drug policies.

My presentation was accepted for the TEDx conference, and for the next 6 weeks, I worked with Nathan McNeil, a friend of mine from college, to cut my 45-minute presentation in half while also including more of my story with Joanne. When I originally gave the presentation at the coffee shop to the group of community leaders, I didn't talk about my experiences as a foster mom. I only shared what I'd learned about addiction and why prohibition causes so much additional harm on so many fronts. Nathan strongly encouraged me to include not only what I learned, but the story that led me there. I'll forever be grateful for that advice as well as Joanne's incredible courage to let me tell her story in such a public way.

TEDX

Before I knew it, it was Valentine's Day 2019, the day of the TEDx conference. I woke up early and put on the outfit I laid out the night before of skinny jeans, a pink ruffled blouse, and a dark green jacket. Fashion has always been my nemesis, and this simple ensemble took me several shopping trips and numerous texts to friends to put together. In just a few hours I would fulfill a dream. Thomas, my husband, encouraged me to relax as I ran through my presentation slides one last time. The doorbell rang as the babysitter arrived to keep our boys. Preparation time was over. This was it.

Thomas and I drove to downtown Jackson, Mississippi, a few miles east of my childhood home at Loden Place. After parking, we parted ways and Thomas found a seat in the auditorium of The Two Museums while I headed upstairs to the green room. I wanted to focus and was worried that I'd get rattled if I saw anyone I knew beforehand. Once I was sure the conference had started, I slipped into the auditorium and found a seat next to several of the other speakers. Before long, it was my turn. Microphone secure, battery pack clipped to my jeans pocket, the remote to change my presentation slides in hand, I walked onto the stage and into the spotlight. Taking a deep breath, I spent the next 20 minutes sharing my unlikely journey as a conservative Christian foster mom who changed my mind on the best way to approach drugs and addiction with a pro-life ethic.

After the overwhelmingly positive feedback from attendees at the TEDx event, it was clear there was something special happening, and I founded End It For Good as a 501(c)3 non-profit that year. Over the summer and fall, Angela Mallette and I drove all over Mississippi hosting book discussions together. I met Angela when she came to one of my first discussions after hearing about it from a coworker, and she became my friend, then volunteer co-host, then End It For Good team member. That fall I also got connected to Brett Montague through James Moore, and Brett helped coordinate the most successful event to date, with 120 leaders attending in Hattiesburg, MS. Brett later joined our team as well and serves as End It For Good's CEO today. No one succeeds alone. Angela, Brett, and many others worked to spark a movement around an idea we each became convinced could change the world.

The video of my TEDx Talk aired publicly in the middle of our event series that summer, exactly 2 years after the first book discussion I hosted, and it catapulted the movement forward.

From the beginning, our mission has been to invite people to support approaches to drugs that prioritize life and the opportunity to thrive. We envision a world where drug production, distribution, and use are approached as health issues rather than criminal justice matters. End It For Good's team continues working to bring that world about. But as you might imagine, it's an uphill climb.

CHAPTER 26

MORE THAN YOU MIGHT THINK

This winding driveway is so familiar. Turning off Clinton Boulevard, I pass the entry gates into the seminary campus. The little white house I was born in used to be on the right, but it was taken down when they built the bookstore that stands today. In front of me is the chapel. When I was young, our church met here for about a year during the construction of our new building in a neighboring town. To the left is a two-story large white house used for out-of-town guests that my grandparents stayed in when they came to visit us. There was no room at Loden Place, but the seminary campus is less than a mile away from my childhood home so it kept them close. As I pass the white house and come around the back side of the chapel, I look for a parking place in the main lot. On one side is an open field where my brothers and I came every week growing up to play soccer with other homeschooled kids. I was one of the youngest, and my strongest memories of those afternoons are getting the wind knocked out of me by a ball to the stomach, and swinging on a nearby swing set with my best friend, Elizabeth. We did a lot more swinging than we did playing.

Beyond the field are the on-campus apartments. The first time I saw the movie *Swiss Family Robinson* was in one of those apartments while Mom helped one of her best friends through a home birth in the next room. We didn't have money for a babysitter and Dad was at work, so we kids just came along. On the other side of the parking lot is a long building filled with classrooms and a gymnasium. The first time I tasted a caramel apple was at a fall carnival in this gym. Later, I spent many hours here babysitting for numerous seminary functions. Across the street from the main campus is the seminary's counseling center where I first stepped into a therapist's office and asked for help as I tried to process losing both of my parents. This campus, where I was born, has been part of my life in so many ways, through so many seasons.

But today I'm here on behalf of End It For Good, speaking to a group of students who are taking a class on addictions because they're studying to become therapists. Just a few steps away from the room I used to babysit in, I set up my slides and greet students. Half the class period I spend sharing what I learned that changed my mind about the best way to approach drugs and addiction, and the other half I spend listening to the students share their feedback on those ideas.

This summer will mark 6 years since the first book discussion, and even though End It For Good has now grown to six team members, we've kept our focus on what made those book discussions so impactful. We invite people into a respectful conversation, giving them research and stories to spark their curiosity, and then we listen to their thoughts.

After I finish my presentation today, one student comments that he has a background very similar to mine. Although the idea of ending prohibition makes sense to him now, he continues, he can't see how it's possible to turn the tide away from incarceration and criminalization when so many conservative Christians like us support it. "It seems like an impossible mountain to climb," he says sadly. He's right that it does seem impossible. At first glance. But if you were a shadow next to me over the last six years through the book discussions and End It For Good's birth and growth, you would feel much more hopeful. As I've listened to several thousand people share their thoughts on ending prohibition and moving towards solutions that prioritize life, health, and safety, it's clear that a lot more people want to scale this mountain than you might think, and that number is growing every day.

YOU TOO?

After my first newspaper article on the issue came out, one of the email responses I got came from a stranger who I later learned is a successful attorney from my parents' generation. In his email, he shared that he's also a conservative Christian Mississippian, and he went on to lay out 7 numbered points as to why making drugs legal for adults would fix so many problems.

He said something else that has echoed through my mind ever since. He told me he's never actually put his thoughts on it down before. He's just been telling his wife about it for years until he saw my article. I'm convinced, based on the last few years of publicly talking about how we handle drugs and addiction, that a large swath of the population is like this man. They quietly agree with something close to where I've landed, but they never talk about it. Most of the people they know don't even realize what they think because it's not exactly a topic that just pops up over lunch. That attorney is far from the only person I've talked to who holds a different opinion privately from what people might assume.

One afternoon I was having coffee with a man who works for the criminal justice system. I asked him what he thought law enforcement officers might think about making more drugs legal. He smiled and said, "Let's find out," as he motioned to someone behind me. I turned around as a man in his 60s in a police uniform walked up to our table. The two men shook hands as old friends. "So," the man having coffee with me said to the officer, "We're discussing the old Mary Jane. What do you think we should do with it?" The officer didn't miss a beat before responding, "Might as well legalize it. Everyone's using it anyway."

Another law enforcement officer who's now a sheriff attended one of the book discussions and came up to me afterward to say that his career had convinced him that marijuana is not a gateway drug, but the prosecution of marijuana is a gateway to a destroyed life.

At one of the discussions I hosted while completing the paperwork for End It For Good to become a nonprofit, the first person in the door was an older man. The first words out of his mouth, as I walked up to introduce myself, were, "I've been waiting 50 years for this!" He explained that when marijuana was criminalized he knew it would be a disaster, and finally we were talking about that disaster out loud.

I wonder what would happen if all the people who privately support a different approach to drugs would say so publicly?

Some people, like the ones above, already agree quietly that change is needed and just need an opportunity to speak it. Some of them may only want change in marijuana policy, while others agree on the big picture of shifting away from prohibition and towards allowing adults to have a broader range of legal options if they choose to use drugs. But even more promising to me is a growing group of people who are experiencing what I did and are actually *changing* their minds. After one presentation that I gave at a Rotary Club, the president of the club came up to me and said, "The whole way through your presentation I was telling myself 'There's no way she's going to say legalization.' And then you did. And you know…it does make good sense."

An engineering manager attended an End It For Good event, and during the audience feedback he said, "When I came tonight, I supported the war on drugs. Now…I'm not so sure."

A man who works with a sheriff's department in Louisiana came to two different events. At the second one he said, "The first time I came and heard the presentation I thought you were nuts." Everyone laughed, because there were people at that moment who thought that very thing. Then he continued, "But now, I think you're onto something."

People across the political and religious spectrum are learning something new and catching a vision for how *everyone* gets more of the world they want with drug policies that reduce harm rather than increase it.

POLICY CHANGES

As I've said before, my heart changed about people and my mind changed about policy. These are the same two things I hope will happen across our culture and country. They can go together, as they have for me, but it's important to note that they don't have to. On the policy front, we might agree on some changes but not all changes.

The first step on the policy front could be to stop advocating for new laws that continue down the same failed path. A police chief told me that the criminal justice system has a very narrow scope of usefulness, and we've come to rely on it for everything that's wrong in the world. When it's used for problems it's not designed to solve, we get bad outcomes. He also told me all of us have "positional opportunity." We have influence specific to our identity, profession, or experiences. Stewarding our positional opportunity wisely is crucial so we don't advocate for knee-jerk reactions to complex problems.

Another change that I think could significantly reduce harm would be for the federal government to deschedule marijuana and allow states to make their own decisions about whether to make it legal or not. Another change would be for states that don't have legal access to open the door to medical or adult use. That doesn't mean I'm thrilled about marijuana. It just means that if it's done well, the underground market and the unnecessary incarceration of consumers will decline. There's still a lot of work to do to reduce harm from marijuana even after it's legal, but at least we've stopped the additional harm of prohibition.

Beyond marijuana, there are other policy changes we might agree on. States could make drug testing products legal so that people can know if the drug they're about to use is contaminated with something like fentanyl. States can also shift resources from arrest and incarceration toward funding for mental health and addiction treatment services.

Another way to make a big impact would be making drug possession a misdemeanor instead of a felony. Even though I don't think it's helpful to arrest people for drug possession (period), I can certainly see the value of this middle ground. If we want a viable workforce and people able to support themselves, we can't keep handing out felonies like they're no big deal, when they cripple a person's employment opportunities for the rest of their lives.

States could make psychedelic drugs legal for medical use as well. Clinical trials are showing incredible promise for psychedelic treatment to help people struggling with mental health issues like anxiety, depression, and PTSD, as well as for people with substance use disorders.

Allowing doctors to prescribe opioids to people who need them or people who are addicted and at risk of using the contaminated street supply would be a way to help pain patients as well as keep addicted people alive and under medical care. This would require a huge sea change away from the demonization of doctors and prescription opioids, but the alternative is much worse. Cutting people off from healthcare at the moment they need it most, and sending them to a street drug supply full of fentanyl makes absolutely no sense.

HEART CHANGES

Aside from policy change, there will be people whose hearts change. They might learn about the suffering that drives addiction and be moved to compassion instead of judgment. That empathy may not change their mind on policy, but it might change their behavior, families, faith communities, and neighborhoods in numerous ways. Heart change even without policy change is really important and can lead to all sorts of good things.

In the treatment arena, places like Above and Beyond Family Recovery Center in Chicago, under the visionary leadership of Dan Hostetler, are offering evidence-based outpatient treatment built around dignity and respect for the people they serve and the stories they have. No policy will ever make anyone see the value of another human being, but people like Dan are building that value into the culture of their work and witnessing fantastic results from it.

A heart change is all that's needed for someone to offer a listening ear instead of wary silence to a friend whose family member is entering treatment for the sixth time. You don't need a legislator to give you permission to volunteer with a nonprofit offering hope and dignity to people whose addictions have taken almost everything from them. No policy is going to make your church any more ready than it is right now to be a safe place for people to be known, loved, belong, and heal. Facilitating deep relationships is part of preventing addiction, supporting people who are on that journey, and empowering recovery. You can pick up the phone right now and call your local jail and find out how to lead a Bible study or life skills class for incarcerated people. You can volunteer or drop off resources at a local transition home for people trying to maintain their sobriety after treatment. You can send a text on the anniversary of an overdose death, letting their loved ones know you're thinking of them on that hard day. Changed hearts can inspire changed lives in so many ways.

ON THE SAME TEAM

Whether you want heart change, policy change, both or neither, we can be friends and have a respectful dialogue. We are on the same team. That's an especially important truth to highlight for my fellow Christians.

Just because I've come to believe that allowing adults to have legal access to a broader range of drugs is the approach that best aligns with my conservative values and my Christian conviction about the sanctity of life, it doesn't mean every conservative or Christian has to agree. For Christians, no one's conscience should be bound on an issue like this that isn't central to saving faith in Jesus Christ. We can agree on matters of faith and disagree on public policy. We might even agree on some policy changes without agreeing on all of them. My deeper hope for the faith community is for us to catch a fresh vision for the role we can play as a place of support, community, hope, and healing for people who struggle with addictions and their loved ones. They're in our pews today, and no law is in the way of us responding well. This goes for addictions to legal drugs like alcohol too.

I've lost count of how many people I've talked to whose spouse or parent is an alcoholic, and they're heartbroken that their church or family or social circles turn a blind eye, unsure of what to do so they just ignore the problem. It's been easier to ignore addictions to illegal drugs because people are less likely to talk about a loved one engaging in something that's been labeled a crime. Even when people do share, it's easy to focus on the criminal activity as the main problem, instead of the core of the addiction being the main problem. The core problem is a whole lot harder to sort out. Maybe we've relied on the law so much with drugs because it's just easier. It gives us a diversion from facing the deep, hard underlying drivers of addiction. The problems remain, though, and the people affected are desperate for others to bear their burdens with them. So how *do* we respond well to what we know now? My mom gave me a glimpse when I was eleven.

CHAPTER 27

SMALL BIG THINGS

The sun slants through the blinds as my ostrich feather duster moves back and forth along them. It's been almost three years since the armed robbery next door. We still have a changing carousel of neighbors at Loden Place, but not much else has changed. Dad still works at Mt. Salus Christian School, Mom homeschools me and my three brothers, and we're still our church's janitors. It takes about 4 ½ hours for our family to clean the church, which we usually do on Saturday afternoons. None of us kids have ever played organized sports, so Saturdays are wide open. Mom cooks dinner for us in the church kitchen after we finish cleaning, and then around 7:00 pm a bunch of kids from the church youth group come to play basketball and volleyball in the gym. Mom and Dad chaperone each week, happy to give their time to something constructive for kids that fosters friendships.

I don't do as many of the janitorial duties as the boys do, so today I'm finishing my last job after two hours, dusting all the classrooms. Mom teaches the four-and-five-year-old Sunday School class, and one of her students, Kaley, lost her mother to cancer a couple of weeks ago.

Amy Brand, a mother Mom's age with three kids younger than us, has lived Mom's worst fear and passed away while her children are still young. Mom didn't know Mrs. Brand personally, but she feels the suffering of her family so deeply. I can't help but wonder what it's like to lose your mom when you still need her. When Mrs. Brand died, I went to her funeral with another family from church. Mom said she just couldn't go. It was too close to her own fears of dying before we're grown.

But she honors Mrs. Brand in her own way. I hang my duster up on the hook Dad installed for it in the janitorial closet, and Mom and I drive out to the Brand's house with several Berenstain Bear books and a game packed in Mom's brown cloth tote bag with an owl embroidered on the side.

For the next several months, we make this drive often when I finish my church cleaning. Kaley, her two older brothers, Mom, and I cram together on their couch while Mom reads them a couple of books before we all play a game together. That's all.

THE OTHER THING THAT LINGERS

With just one hour of quality time every week or two, Mom entered into the Brand family's suffering. By choice. I don't think she had any idea that taking me along would have such deep echoes in my own life today.

What strikes me now, as an adult thinking back on those months, is that no one would've faulted her for just going to the funeral and continuing on with life. Entering into the visible and short-term is what people tend to do best. She took it a step further, looking for the invisible grief, loss, and longing beyond that visible funeral. She put herself in the shoes of this family and let the depth of grief she knew they were feeling wash over her. She couldn't bring Amy back, but she could enter in and shoulder a tiny bit of the burden as her children began building a life without their mom.

My parents saw the world as it really is, full of people who are hurting, struggling, and grieving. Each life is precious to God, longing to be whole. What's visible in their lives is only the tip of the iceberg. Mom and Dad had eyes that lingered on the unseen, seeing more clearly because of it. Opportunities to be a burden bearer abound if we take the time to lean in like they did.

As an adult, Amy's daughter Kaley became a hospice social worker. I hadn't talked to her since those Saturday afternoons 25 years ago, but when she responded to a message I sent while I was writing this book, she began with, "I share the story of your mom coming to read to us often." She was just five years old at the time. Trauma isn't the only thing that lingers. Connection does too.

Mom and Dad didn't measure success by the number of people they impacted. They read Scripture, prayed for direction, and tried to see the opportunities God put in front of them. Mom didn't read to every child who lost a parent. She read to two boys and their little sister. Dad didn't mentor fifty men struggling with addiction, he mentored just one. They didn't try to change the world. They tried to be faithful to the opportunities and people in front of them.

THREE STEPS

If you want to be part of culture or policy change, where do you start? A guest preacher at church mentioned one Sunday that most of us spend too much time trying to figure out "the thing" God wants us to do. Instead, he said, we should consider these three action steps:

1. Look for what's in front of you
2. Learn as much as you can about it
3. Jump in where you can contribute

What is in front of you on this big issue of drugs and addiction? What can you learn about it? Where can you contribute? The way we handle drugs and addiction impacts virtually everyone on the planet in one way or another. There's a role for you in making it better.

GETTING CURIOUS

"Heart change and policy change are only possible as more people have the opportunity to get curious and learn. You don't necessarily have to go talk to your senator or mayor to impact what they do. You can share this book with your neighbor, mother, or boss. You could also get a few people together over dinner and discuss the ideas in it. Details to download a discussion guide are in the back of the book, making a gathering like this simple to host.

Inviting people to learn is vulnerable and a little terrifying sometimes, but it's also vulnerable for them to engage. If we want others to embrace vulnerability and consider new ideas, we have to embrace it first and put the ideas before them with humility. That means I'm not a warrior, and I don't want you to be either. I hope for a movement of bridge-builders. People who engage in respectful dialogue, even when there's disagreement. Shame and blame have not served us well as tools to change the lives of addicted people, and they won't serve us well to influence hearts, minds, or laws. Be a bridge-builder. Help people learn, consider, and engage with ideas they may have discarded previously.

I didn't change my mind overnight – and most other people don't either. We all need time - to learn, think, ask questions, and explore. Your effort to spark curiosity and conversation could save someone's life. Spare someone harm. Help someone heal. That's worth getting out on the skinny branches for. You might not see the impact, but God does, and that's enough.

You might invite one person to read this book and consider the ideas offered here. You might help your faith community better understand addiction. You might volunteer or donate or pray or mentor. I don't know what's in front of you, but I hope this book has given you some new ideas and lit a flame inside you to find your way to contribute. The impact of current drug policy is vast, which means the potential impact of better drug policy is also vast.

If you want to see heart change, the sky's the limit. Inviting people to get curious is as easy as telling them about Rat Park and the true drivers of addiction.

STRONGER THAN YOU THINK

If you care about policy change but it seems too daunting, remember this: The only voice louder than lobbyists and special interest groups is the voters themselves. If we tell our elected officials we want tough laws and harsh penalties, that's what we'll get. If we communicate instead that we only want incarceration used when it improves public safety, that's what we'll get. Whether the elected person is a judge, mayor, sheriff, prosecutor, state legislator, or leader in Congress, they all need the support of voters to keep their seat. The voice of voters can change the votes of our leaders, but only if we're willing to speak up. If you think the general public is afraid of change, an elected official feels that times ten. If we want change, it's our job as voters to advocate for it. Our leaders are looking to their constituents to determine which policies they should support. Open the door for your leaders. Chances are a lot of them quietly agree, but they need public support before they can act. You can give it to them. That's not to say it's easy.

Most of us don't want to be pioneers. Pioneers tend to get slaughtered. We want to be settlers. They come in later and prosper. But real people's lives are at stake here. In some states, pioneers are needed. In others, the pioneering work is transitioning into settler work. Either way, it'll take some courage to engage.

Our culture has been swept along in the river of punitive approaches to drugs for a century. When you put your feet under you and stand up, you'll likely feel the force of the current. And when you try to move upstream and channel the river in a different direction, it may take more effort than you anticipated. But this is the path to change.

Every leap forward in human history has come because a small group of people was willing to break from the status quo and say, "There's a better way and I'm going to work toward it." They break with convention and follow their convictions. Drug prohibition will end and health-centered approaches will be adopted when we reach a tipping point of enough people who say, "I'm going to work toward it." People who use drugs aren't the only ones responsible for their choices. Those of us who influence our cultural and legislative approach to drugs are too. We can be part of better solutions. If we continue down the same path we're on today, one million people will die of overdose in the next ten years. Peter Muyshondt, a police chief who's now publicly advocating for ending drug prohibition, told me the reason he's risking his career over this issue is because it won't change until we take the risks. If people years ago had spoken up we could've saved so many lives, he says. If we don't want to wake up in ten or fifty years and be in the same predicament, we have to speak up now.

Will it require dedication? Will it seem like an uphill climb? Absolutely. But the steepest climbs end with the best view…and are accomplished like every other journey: one step at a time.

If I have breath in my lungs today, it is because God's purposes for me here on this earth are not complete. If you're alive today, his purposes for you aren't complete either. Maybe you're struggling with addiction or walking with someone who is. Maybe you lost a loved one to overdose and long to prevent others from walking through the same valley. Maybe your loved one is incarcerated and you feel like you're sitting in that cell with them, day after day, year after year. Or maybe you're someone like me, who didn't know there were things you didn't know about drugs and addiction.

The train wreck and Mom and Dad's deaths helped me see what's true about the brevity of life. Every breath is a gift. Joanne and James Moore and many others showed me that every person has a story.

OUR TURN

Recently I was speaking to a group of master's students. Each had a chance to share their feedback, and the last person to speak was Amanda, a girl in the back row with long brown hair. She started off by saying that my presentation made her really sad. She shared about her chaotic childhood as her dad struggled with addiction to numerous drugs including heroin, trying to hide his addiction because of the shame of stigma and fear of arrest, rather than reaching out for help. Her dad had recently passed away from drug-related causes. She finished with, "I feel sad because if we'd done what you're talking about a long time ago, my childhood might have been very different, and my dad might still be alive."

We can't change Amanda's story, but we have an opportunity to make changes today that will change the stories of thousands of little girls yet to be born. Changed hearts, minds, and policies can change the next generation, leaving them a safer, healthier world. The heart that drew me to foster care is the same heart that led me to start End It For Good. We can celebrate the sanctity of life in innocent children *and* in adults whose broken hearts and bad decisions make it a little harder sometimes. I didn't change my mind about legal access to drugs in spite of my pro-life values. I changed my mind because of them.

A criminal justice approach to drugs had a beginning, and it can have an end. People before us chose the current path, and we can choose a better one.

AFTERWORD

For me, the hardest part of writing this book has been knowing that once it hits the press, I'll keep growing. And changing. And learning. And seeing more clearly than I do today. And that means there will be things in this book that I wish I could change one day. I could have waited another 20 years and written a more perfect book, but I chose to share my journey with where I am today. It's not the final word, but if it can help change the course of even a few people's lives for the better, then it's worth it. I'm still learning, and I hope you are too. Let's stay curious, growing, and taking action together.

On the first day of writing this book, I read these verses from Psalm 145 in Eugene Peterson's The Message: "God is good to one and all; everything he does is soaked through with grace." My life has been soaked through with God's grace through the sacrifice of his Son, Jesus, to cover all the judgment, anger, bitterness, jealousy, and hard-heartedness of my soul. I hope, in this book, you catch a glimpse of God's grace too. It's there for each of us, a free gift as we surrender to King Jesus and find our true home as His beloved child. If your journey is marked by grief, he weeps with you. If you're rejoicing, he sings over you. His arms are open as he invites you to come in out of the cold and find rest in Him.

On the last day of writing this book - today - I spent 2 hours in a prison in south Mississippi. It's been six years since that very first *Chasing the Scream* book discussion at Corner Bakery with twelve people, and I've now led thirty-five similar events in many different cities and towns. A woman came to one of those events who works for the Mississippi Humanities Council. She read *Chasing the Scream* and thought it would be a great book to add to their reading list for several book clubs they sponsor in prisons. This newly started club at a prison in south Mississippi, led by a professor from the University of Southern Mississippi, picked it as their next read. They spent three sessions discussing the book with the professor, then invited me to join them for their 4th and final session on it.

The professor, Dr. Joe Peterson, meets me in the parking lot so we can walk in together. While I wait for him to get materials out of his car, I'm struck by how many birds I hear singing, even though there are no trees anywhere inside the sprawling prison compound consisting of drab buildings, guard towers, fencing topped with razor wire, and empty grassy areas. The professor questions one of the prison employees about the birds as we walk in, noticing the same thing I do. "The men feed them," the employee responds with a smile. They're one of the only glimpses of the natural world that these men have access to.

We walk through security, the professor having to leave all his dry erase markers with one of the guards after a new policy was instituted two weeks ago. Apparently a visitor brought in markers with drugs inside in place of ink, so no markers are allowed anymore. We're led through a labyrinth of halls, rooms, doors, sidewalks and grassy yards, passing old men in wheelchairs and young men who look like they're still teenagers. Seeing people in prison who are old enough and frail enough to be wheelchair-bound is startling. I guess the mugshots we see on the news are when they're going in. What happens thirty years later is out of sight.

Men are mowing the grass, cooking lunch, waiting to be seen by medical staff in the infirmary, and practicing a keyboard for chapel services the next morning. We finally come to the room we'll be meeting in. About twenty-five men join us for the discussion. The first one I meet has spent the last twenty-five years in prison. Guessing at his age, he's likely spent more than half his life here. In come others. Some of them are older, some younger, but all of them are only eligible for this book group because of stellar behavior while incarcerated.

Joe starts the class and introduces me before asking me to share a little bit about my own journey on the issue of drugs and addiction as well as the work End It For Good does. I do, but as quickly as I can I move into the reason I've driven two and a half hours to spend ninety minutes with these men. I want to know what they think. They're serving time for many different reasons, but I know some of them are here on drug charges. I've led discussions on these issues with several thousand people now, but never with people actively serving time in prison for the very policies End It For Good is working to change. I structure the discussion the same way I do with free people, everyone getting one or two minutes to share their thoughts before "passing the mic" to the person next to them.

When people share their thoughts, they're letting you into their world. That's an honor that I deeply appreciate. Hearing the stories of their lives that inform those thoughts is even more special.

For the rest of our time, the men share what they think about the ideas in *Chasing the Scream*. Many of the same ideas are shared in this book, from a different point of view. It's enlightening but also heartbreaking as I listen. One man, who can't be older than thirty-five, is serving a sixty-year sentence for selling an amount of cocaine equal to the weight of a golf ball. He has no violent offenses on his record. Another one, whose deep voice fills the room, is serving thirty years for selling marijuana - something that people are making legal profits off of in Mississippi today. Two other men come up to me afterward to share how they connected with my experience as a foster parent, because their own children are in foster care while they're in prison.

We all have choices. These men made choices and are paying dearly for them. But the rest of us have choices too. We have chosen the policies and culture we have today, and we can choose something better for tomorrow. Juan Francisco Torres Landa Ruffo is a Mexican attorney trained at Harvard Law School who has been working for the last decade to defund cartels through making more drugs legal in Mexico. "I'm a runner," he told me a couple of years ago. "I've run marathons, but this is the longest marathon I've ever run." It won't be easy, and it won't always be exciting. There will be some backward motion as people wield fear and encourage us to continue the old ways of "lock 'em up." It feels good, even if it doesn't fix the problem.

But this work–creating policy and culture change that aligns with what we know about addiction and what we know can reduce suffering–is worth it. I walked out of that prison today,

AFTERWORD

got in my van, and drove two and a half hours back home. I picked my kids up from school, went to Costco, and ate dinner with my family. Mundane, everyday things. Things the men I spent time with today can't do. Things some of them haven't done in decades, and others won't get to do for decades to come. It doesn't have to be this way for some of them. We may not be able to change their lives, but we can fix broken policies before another generation is escorted into prison or carried into a funeral home unnecessarily. These are real people made in the image of God that we're speaking up for. In whatever way you see a need for change, go for it. One life, one law, one step at a time. It's worth it.

ACKNOWLEDGMENTS

There are so many people who made this book possible. The first is Joanne, who has courageously said "yes" every time I've asked to share our story publicly. You are the hero in this book, Joanne, and meeting you is one of the most impactful experiences of my life. Thank you for letting me really see you. You're remarkable.

Second is Thomas, my husband. Just writing his name here brings tears to my eyes. Thomas has taken this four-year book journey along with me. When I've been paralyzed, afraid, overwhelmed, uncertain, exhausted, and empty, he has pulled me along until my sails caught the wind again. I finished this book because of his unwavering support and encouragement.

Thank you to the passionate, talented people I've had the privilege of working with on the End It For Good team: Brett Montague, Angela Mallette, Jennifer Allen, Jane Clair Tyner, and Andrea Thornton.

Next is my brother Joel, an entrepreneur and prolific idea man who dropped by my office one afternoon in January 2020 to tell me his latest great idea - I should write a book! I had the pleasure of meeting author Johann Hari in 2018, and I sent him Joel's ridiculous idea to shoot down. He replied back, "You must must must do it!" It's good we don't know how hard things will be before we actually do them. Thank you both for your steadfast encouragement.

The people whose stories are included in this book are only a fraction of the people who shared their stories with me on this journey. Whether or not your story is included, every story shaped me and this book.

To the current and former law enforcement officers who shared: Bill Spearn, Chris Freeze, Diane Goldstein, Henrik Orye, Howard Wooldridge, James Moore, Matthew Garvin, Neil Woods, Peter Muyshondt, and Suzanne Sharkey, thank you for your courage in the line of duty and your courage to advocate for improvements to policing.

To the people who shared from your professional perspectives on policy, medical care, and addiction: Armando Santacruz, Dr. Branden Henry, Dr. Bruce Alexander, Catherine Hagwood, Clark Neily, Cliff Osbon, Colleen Cowles, Crispin Blunt MP, Dan Hostetler, Daniel Snyder, David Hairston, Gretchen Bergman, Hanna Dershowitz, Ismail Ali, Jacob Rich, Judge Jamie Jameson, Dr. John Adams, Dr. John Hey, John Shinholser, Juan Francisco Torres Landa Ruffo, Kevin Armstrong, Melody Worsham, Michael Crouch, Pauline Rogers, Robert Legge, Sara Scott, Stefany Campos, Steve Rolles, Thomas Byars, Timothy King, and Dr. William Sansing.

To the people who shared your personal stories of impact from how we approach drugs and addiction today, as well as those who shared the story of changing your own minds about the best path forward: Alison Saucier, Amanda Hamilton, Amanda Stokes, Amy Ard, Austin Davies, Bridgette Walton,

ACKNOWLEDGMENTS

Cher Matthews, Christi Berrong-Barber, Christian Chism, Clay Finchum, Daniel Keeling, Denise Herrington, Diannee Carden Glenn, Floyd Rodgers Jr., Gabi Raines, Ian Biss, Jessie Dunleavy, Jim Smith, Josefina, Joseph Rubin, Juanita Blevins, Ken Flynt, Kristin Hatten, Lauren McGraw, Lee Malouf, Lisa Sublett, Lizz Lambert, Maria Alexander, Michele Tackett, Nikki Williams, Payton, Shelby Wilson, Tim Bridges, and Will Morgan, I am honored and humbled that you entrusted your stories to me. Thank you.

Thank you to Kaley, Jarred, and Corbin Brand for letting me share a snapshot from your story.

Juan Cloy, Nicole McNamee, Jonathan Lee, Pam Shaw, David Pharr, and Tim Mask are the chain of people whose efforts gave me the TEDx stage. Thank you.

Jene' Barranco helped me map out the book's structure and get started. Karen White listened to me tell the whole story so I could learn to write in my speaking voice. Phillip Holmes offered interview transcription and has been a source of ideas since the beginning.

This book touches numerous topics people go to school for years to understand. Thank you Dr. Jefferson Parker, Dr. Jeffrey Singer, Jeremiah Mosteller and Leonard Gilroy for reading drafts for accuracy, and Marilyn Tinnin and Lloyd Robertson for reading drafts for clarity.

My parents Dennis and Sharon Bomgaars gave me a childhood filled with belonging, love, laughter, and purpose. Maybe most important for this journey, they showed me how to be curious. Until we meet again, Mom and Dad, thank you. My brothers Micah, Joel, and Daniel, as well as Tommy and Mary Dent and Linda and Kerry Goff have been wonderfully supportive.

To find one steadfast, trustworthy, true friend is a precious gift. To have many is priceless. Thank you to the circles of women from Providence, Belhaven, Redeemer, Trace Ridge, and the places between who have filled my life with connection and deep friendships.

Jeremy Brown at Throne Publishing helped me see a path to finishing this book, and Liz DeJongh edited it and gave me hope that it might actually be good. Thank you.

This journey has been a deeply spiritual one for me as I see the work of God in a long arc over my life. To my pastors whose teaching throughout my life beckoned me closer to Jesus even when the path was dark: John Reeves, Wade Coleman, Mike Campbell, Elbert McGowan, and now Steve Street. Thank you for being faithful shepherds.

And lastly, if you're reading this you very likely read this book. Thank you for lending your time, mind, and heart to me. Wherever you land on the best path forward with drugs and addiction, I hope you look for what's in front of you, how you can contribute, and dive in.

NOTES

1. Leire Leza, et al., Adverse childhood experiences (ACEs) and substance use disorder (SUD): A scoping review, 221 Drug and Alcohol Dependence 1 (2021); McKenzie Lynn LeTendre & Mark B. Reed, The Effect of Adverse Childhood Experience on Clinical Diagnosis of a Substance Use Disorder: Results of a Nationally Representative Study, 52 Substance Use & Misuse 689 (2017).
2. Bureau of Justice Statistics, Prisoners in 2021 – Statistical Tables, Department of Justice (2022), https://bjs.ojp.gov/library/publications/prisoners-2021-statistical-tables; Helen Fair and Roy Walmsley, World Prison Population List, Institute for Crime & Justice Policy Research (13th eds. 2021), available at https://www.prisonstudies.org/research-publications.
3. Substance Abuse and Mental Health Services Administration, 2021 National Survey on Drug Use and Health, Department of Health and Human Services (2023), https://www.samhsa.gov/data/report/2021-nsduh-detailed-tables.

4. Federal Bureau of Investigation, Incidents Cleared by Offense Category, 2021, U.S. Department of Justice (2022), available at https://crime-data-explorer.app.cloud.gov/pages/downloads
5. Source: Megan E. Slater & Hillel R. Alpert, Apparent Per Capita Alcohol Consumption: National, State, and Regional Trends, 1977–2021, National Institute on Alcohol Abuse and Alcoholism (2023), available at https://www.niaaa.nih.gov/publications/surveillance-reports.
6. Ecclesiastes 1:9
7. https://monitoringthefuture.org/wp-content/uploads/2022/12/mtf2022.pdf
8. Milja Heikkinen, et al.,Real-world effectiveness of pharmacological treatments of opioid use disorder in a national cohort, 117 Addiction 1683 (2022); Kimberly D. Brunisholz, et al., Trends in abstinence and retention associated with implementing a Medication Assisted Treatment program for people with opioid use disorders using a Collective Impact approach, 14 Progress in Community Health Partnerships 43 (2020); Jun Ma, et al., Effects of medication-assisted treatment on mortality among opioids users: a systematic review and meta-analysis, 24 Molecular Psychiatry 1868 (2019).

ABOUT THE AUTHOR

Christina Dent is the Founder and President of End It For Good, a nonprofit that invites people to support approaches to drugs that prioritize life and the opportunity to thrive. Born and raised in Jackson, Mississippi, she received a bachelor's degree in Biblical Studies from Belhaven University and has spent much of her adult life in volunteer ministry leadership at her church. She supported a criminal justice approach to drugs and addiction until experiences as a foster parent sparked curiosity about whether health-centered approaches might produce outcomes more in line with her conservative Christian values. Christina presented the research and experiences that changed her mind in favor of a health-centered approach in a TEDx Talk and went on to found End It For Good. She writes and speaks across the country, inviting others to learn about the root causes of drug-related harm, and to pursue lasting solutions, however unexpected they may be. Her passion for a better path forward with drugs and addiction is the same passion that led her to foster care. She desires to see children, families, and communities thrive.

You can connect with her through email at curious@enditforgood.com or social media @christinabdent.

ABOUT END IT FOR GOOD

End It For Good began as a passion project of Christina Dent in 2017, to invite more people to consider shifting away from a criminal justice approach to drugs and addiction and towards a health-centered one. As more and more people engaged, a movement was born. End It For Good became a 501(c)3 nonprofit in 2019 and has a growing team educating citizens, advocates, and policymakers to elevate health-centered approaches to drugs and addiction. We believe this shift could dramatically reduce crime, overdose deaths, and the destabilization of families, getting us closer to our ultimate goal - a world where more children, families, and communities thrive.

If you want to connect with me or the work of End It For Good, email curious@enditforgood.com or visit www.enditforgood.com.

To learn more about our work and join the movement, visit www.enditforgood.com and connect with us on social media @enditforgoodms and in our End It For Good Together group on Facebook.

SPARK CURIOSITY

The best way to share the ideas in this book is to invite a few people to read it together. I've created a discussion guide for you that's simple and follows the same approach I used when I first started inviting people into this conversation. Go to www.enditforgood.com/curious to download it, and set a date for your first one. If my schedule allows, I'd love to pop in virtually and meet your group. Email me at curious@enditforgood.com for availability.

The majority of proceeds from book sales go right back into the work of End It For Good, inviting even more people to consider health-centered approaches to drugs that prioritize life and the opportunity to thrive. Whether you host a discussion or simply gift a copy of Curious to a friend, you're helping this movement towards life and health grow. Big changes begin with small actions.

With Hope,
Christina

Made in the USA
Columbia, SC
17 December 2023